fast fat quarter
baby quilts

with M'Liss Rae Hawley

MAKE DARLING DOLL,
INFANT, & TODDLER QUILTS
◆ BONUS LAYETTE SET

C&T PUBLISHING

Text copyright © 2009 by M'Liss Rae Hawley

Artwork copyright © 2009 by C&T Publishing, Inc.

Publisher: Amy Marson

Creative Director: Gailen Runge

Editors: Cynthia Bix and Kesel Wilson

Technical Editors: Ann Haley and Teresa Stroin

Copyeditor/Proofreader: Wordfirm Inc.

Cover/Book Designer: Christina D. Jarumay

Production Coordinator: Tim Manibusan

Illustrator: Mary Flynn

Photography by Christina Carty-Francis and Diane Pedersen
of C&T Publishing, Inc., unless otherwise noted

Cover and Author Photographs by Michael Stadler

Published by C&T Publishing, Inc., P.O. Box 1456,
Lafayette, CA 94549

Library of Congress Cataloging-in-Publication Data

Hawley, M'Liss Rae,

Fast, fat quarter baby quilts with M'Liss Rae Hawley : make darling
doll, infant, & toddler quilts : bonus layette set / M'Liss Rae Hawley.

p. cm.

Summary: "A guide to selecting and working with fat quarter,
large scale, and directional print fabrics to create successful infant,
toddler, and doll quilts. Projects are designed for all levels, great for
beginners and first time quilters"--Provided by publisher.

ISBN 978-1-57120-527-8 (paper trade : alk. paper)

1. Patchwork--Patterns. 2. Quilting--Patterns. 3. Children's quilts
I. Title.

TT835.H3457 2009

746.46'041--dc22

2008041961

Printed in China

10 9 8 7 6 5 4 3 2

ACKNOWLEDGMENTS

I would like to gratefully thank the following people and companies who share my vision, enthusiasm, and love of quilting—and who contributed to the creation of this book.

C&T Publishing: Amy Marson, Gailen Runge, Cynthia Bix, Kesel Wilson, Christina Jarumay, Tim Manibusan, Janet Levin, Ann Haley, Sandy Peterson, Lisa Fulmer Bruce, and all the staff who continue to create wonderful books

Electric Quilt

Hoffman Fabrics

OLFA

Quilters Dream Batting

Thank you to Steiff, Inc., for allowing us to use their adorable bears and rabbit for our photo shoots.

Thank you to Peggy Johnson — the "Keeper of the Blocks." With the Electric Quilt software, Peggy helped draft the patterns in the book. Thank you!

And thank you to my friends Vicki, Peggy, Susie, John, and Louise, and to my sister, Erin, for the last-minute help with piecing and bindings!

A special thank-you to my contributors, an amazing group of dedicated and talented quilters. They continue to inspire me in many ways.

Finally, thank you to Michael, Adrienne, and Alexander — my family.

DEDICATION

I lovingly dedicate this book
to all mothers and babies
—and especially to my mother,
Josephine Walsh Frandsen,
and my children,
Alexander and Adrienne.

contents

INTRODUCTION

Fun and colorful fat-quarter quilts and children go together as naturally as chocolate chip cookies and milk. So maybe it was inevitable that I would create a book devoted to babies' and children's quilts made from fat quarters!

Since my very first fat-quarter quilt book was published, one comment I've gotten so often from readers is: "I love fat quarters, and the first quilt I made was from your book, for my friend's (or sister's or niece's) baby!" That's so often true: people who love the idea of making a quilt but have never tried it frequently start off by making a baby quilt. They're fun and quick to make, and they give us an excuse to choose and use so many bright, charming, and interesting fabrics, partly because the patterns require small amounts of yardage. You'll notice that the quilts and smaller projects in this book feature bright, modern fabrics that fit right in with today's new ideas and attitudes about colors and motifs for babies' and children's rooms.

This book offers something for quilters on every level, from beginners to more experienced quilters looking for a small-size, quick project that allows them to exercise their creativity.

I've designed six fun-and-easy fat-quarter quilts—three crib-size, and three child- or lap-size. In addition, there are super-simple, super-speedy small projects like my *Welcome Home Layette Set* and—a special bonus—charming doll quilts to make as companions to the larger quilts or as a gift for a young child. You'll also find a one-yard or panel quilt that's perfect to make for a last-minute gift from Grandma or Auntie, or for charity.

And, by the way, when *I* become a grandmother, I'll be sure to let you know!

quiltmaking with fat quarters

If you're about to make your first quilt, the information I've provided in this chapter will help you feel comfortable with basic quilting terms and tools, fabrics, and design concepts. But even if you're experienced, the information that follows is a great refresher course and provides inspiration and ideas for selecting fabrics that make a baby or child's quilt so special and charming.

REFRESHER COURSE: ANATOMY OF A QUILT

A quilt is basically a three-layer fabric "sandwich" composed of a quilt top (usually made up of different blocks), batting, and a backing.

A *block* is a section of the quilt that forms a self-contained design—either literal, such as stars or pinwheels, or abstract. A block is usually square, but it may also be a rectangle or other geometric shape.

Units are smaller pieces that are sewn together to make a pieced block. All the blocks in this book are pieced. Units may be squares or rectangles cut from a single piece of fabric, or they may themselves be pieced from smaller squares, as in *Play Time* (page 50), or from rectangles or even triangles.

Lattice strips sometimes separate the blocks, as in *Building Blocks* (page 23). Lattice strips act as a frame to highlight each block. You may sometimes see these strips referred to as *sashing*.

Cornerstones are little squares that appear at the corners of the blocks where the vertical and horizontal lattice strips meet. While they are not essential—the vertical or horizontal lattice can be cut from a single long strip—these squares make a lovely design element and sometimes even create secondary designs with the corners of adjacent blocks. *Building Blocks* (page 23) is a good example of a quilt with cornerstones.

Borders are strips of fabric that surround the quilt top on all four sides, much like a frame surrounds a painting. Some quilts also have a narrow *inner border* (think of a mat in a picture frame). Often this is in an accent color. The wider *outer border*, which completes the overall design, may repeat one of the fabrics in the quilt top. Or it could be a different fabric that coordinates and completes the look.

The *quilt top* is complete when the blocks are sewn together and borders are added.

Batting is a layer of cotton or polyester that is the "filling" of the quilt sandwich.

Backing completes the quilt sandwich. It is usually a single fabric that coordinates with the quilt top.

Quilting is the stitching that secures the three layers together. The stitching may be decorative or strictly utilitarian; it may be done by machine or by hand.

Binding, sewn from narrow fabric strips, finishes the edges of the stitched quilt sandwich.

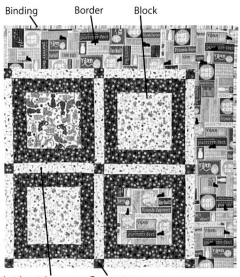

Binding · Border · Block

Lattice strip · Cornerstone

fabric basics

Many quilters say that a quilt or fabric store is really a candy store for grown-ups! When you scan those rainbow bolts of fabric on the shelves, in your favorite catalog, or online, you'll probably agree.

No matter what quilt pattern you decide to make, you will need to choose a variety of fabrics, including a *theme* or *focus* fabric, a *background* fabric, and fabrics for elements such as lattices and cornerstones, as well as borders and binding.

Even though selecting the fabric is one of the most exciting parts of making a quilt, it can also be overwhelming, especially for a beginner. There are just so many wonderful choices out there! Here are some suggestions for an enjoyable—and successful—fabric experience:

■ Because I am a purist, I prefer to use 100% cotton fabrics in my quilts. I recommend that you do too, especially for babies' and children's quilts. Cotton is soft, is easy to work with, wears well, and is very forgiving. In general, I strongly suggest that you stay away from polyester and cotton-polyester blends, which have a tendency to ravel and can be slippery and difficult to handle.

■ Of course, nothing is softer or cuddlier than cotton flannel—a natural choice for the nursery and for children, who love a good snuggle! You can certainly use flannel to make the quilts in this book, like Susie Kincy's *Prehistoric Playtime* (page 47). Some of the small projects, like the *Receiving Blanket* (page 63), are made of flannel. You'll find plenty of adorable flannel prints with whimsical, child-friendly themes to choose from.

■ Prewashing your fabrics, a practice I advocate, will preshrink the fabric, remove any excess finishing chemicals, and make the fabric softer to the touch. Since babies' and children's quilts will be washed over and over again, it's especially important to prewash. And it's crucial to prewash flannel, because it tends to shrink and fray quite a bit. I prewash all new fabric—small pieces in the sink, and ½-yard and larger pieces in the washing machine.

■ Next comes the ironing: straight from the dryer, you can iron fabrics, square them up as described in Squaring Up Your Fabric (page 74), and put them on the shelf in no time. (I'm fortunate because my husband, Michael, irons all my fabric!)

UNDERSTANDING YOUR FABRIC

Cotton fabric is woven so it has a lengthwise and crosswise direction. It helps to understand this so you can best determine how to cut your fabrics for piecing.

The fabric is finished with a tightly woven edge along the two lengthwise sides. This is called the *selvage*. Because selvages are more tightly woven, you may need to trim them off before using the fabric.

The *lengthwise* direction (or lengthwise grain) runs parallel to the selvage. The lengthwise grain has little, if any, give.

The *crosswise* direction (or crosswise grain) runs across the width of the fabric, from selvage to selvage. This grain has a slight bit of give.

Any angle that does not run precisely parallel or perpendicular to the selvage—that is, one that runs on the diagonal of the fabric—is called the *bias* of the fabric. The bias has lots of stretch, so you will want to avoid having this stretchy edge fall on the outside edge of a unit or block.

All yardages for the quilts in this book are based on fabric that is approximately 42″–44″ wide on the bolt and assume a usable width of 40″ after the fabric has been laundered and prepared for cutting.

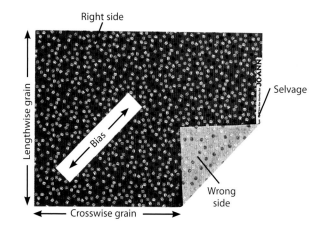

focus on fat quarters

Here's where the real fun begins! To start, you'll need to choose one or more *theme* fabrics—sometimes called *focus* fabrics—that will set the color scheme and tone as well as the design theme for your quilt. I often encourage students, especially first-time quilters, to begin by choosing a multicolor fabric with a medium- to large-scale print that they absolutely love.

WHAT IS A FAT QUARTER?

Unlike a standard ¼ yard of fabric, which is cut across the full width of the fabric and measures 9″ × 42″, a fat quarter is ½ yard of fabric (18″ × 42″) cut in half along the lengthwise grain of the fabric, along the fold. A fat quarter should measure 18″ × 21″.

In reality, when you examine fat-quarter pieces, you may notice slight differences in size, even within the same packet of fabrics. This variation can happen for a number of reasons. Some manufacturers' fabrics are slightly narrower than the industry standard of 42 inches. Some shops consistently cut their fat quarters slightly larger or smaller. Selvages may reduce the usable dimensions.

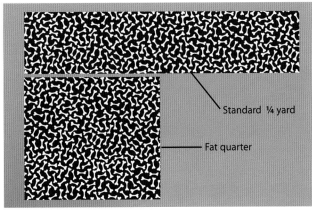

Standard ¼ yard versus fat quarter

What happens after you bring your fabric home can also make a difference in the size of your fat quarters. Prewashing (see Fabric Basics, page 8) can shrink fabric slightly, and the washing machine has a tendency to fray smaller pieces of fabric even more than it does larger ones.

Because of these variables, I've based the patterns in this book on fat quarters that measure 17½″ × 20″ after laundering. I suggest that you measure all your fat quarters after you wash them. Measuring can spare you surprises (and frustration) when you begin cutting. Depending on the usable size of your fat quarters, you may want or need to add additional fat quarters. You may decide to make more or fewer blocks than the instructions call for.

FAT-QUARTER LEFTOVERS

In my previous fat-quarter books, the patterns use all or most of each 17½″ × 20″ fat quarter. In most cases, the quantity of fat quarters and background fabric determines the size of the quilt. But in this book, because most of the quilts are small, only a portion of each fat quarter is used. I wanted to use a variety of fat quarters in order to make each quilt look lively and interesting, and I felt that variety was more important than using up every bit of each fat quarter.

Luckily, there are plenty of creative ways to "use up" the extra fabric. One very special option is to make one of my doll quilts, such as *Play Time* (*pages 53 and 54*) or *Baby Steps* (*page 57*). You could also use the extra fabric for binding, to make a quilt label, or to start another quilt!

EASY FAT-QUARTER PACKETS

Whatever level of quilter you are, precut, prepackaged fat-quarter packets are a great place to start in planning your fat-quarter quilt. Look around! Quilt shops, catalogs, and online sources assemble luscious groupings for our convenience—and delight (see Resources, page 86). You can often find packets with baby or youth themes—perfect for the projects in this book.

These handy collections are the ultimate in reducing your variables. Four to eight beautifully coordinated fat quarters make it effortless for the beginner and the experienced quilter alike to assemble the fabrics for a successful quilt. And if you have extra fat quarters from a packet, you can always use them for one or more of the smaller projects on pages 57–69.

If you want to try creating your own fat-quarter packet, a fabric collection, like my *Meow* (in *I Love Kitties!*, page 23) and *Good Dog* (in *Best Friends*, page 50), is a great way to do it. Because the prints in a collection are designed to harmonize, it's also a good way to select coordinating border and background fabrics for your quilt.

I made *Best Friends* (page 50) using fat quarters from my *Good Dog* fabric collection.

When I'm not buying precut or prepackaged fat quarters, I typically purchase a minimum of ⅝ yard off the bolt. This yardage gives me two fat quarters (one to share with a friend, perhaps) plus a little extra. When I'm choosing fabric for a border, I buy the necessary yardage plus an additional ½ yard in case I wish to include this fabric as a fat quarter too.

making fabric choices

So, where do you begin in making fabric choices for your baby or child's quilt? I often suggest to my students that they select the quilt pattern first; the pattern may bring a specific fabric or theme to mind. Alternative sources of inspiration include the following:

■ **A theme:** For a baby or child's quilt, the delights of childhood itself suggest so many wonderful and varied themes! From pets and farm animals to circuses, trucks, fairies, and twinkling stars—the choice is almost endless. If you're making a quilt for an older child, let his or her interests (in baseball, dolls, butterflies, outer space, or whatever) set the theme. For example, Anastasia Riordan's *Dance Baby Dance* (page 27) is built around a theme of ballet shoes and dancing fairies. You can pick traditional nursery prints or more contemporary, stylized motifs—the sky's the limit. *Let the theme direct your choice of fabric.*

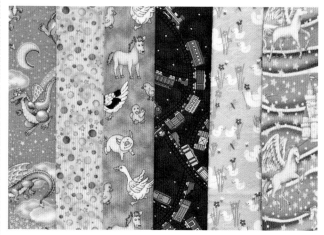

Examples of childhood theme fabrics

■ **A background or border fabric:** If you see a potential border fabric that captures your imagination, this may be the place to start. For example, in my quilt *Best Friends* (page 50), my *Good Dog* border fabric with its dog motif inspired the colors in the rest of the quilt. Generally, a border fabric with a dark background may dictate different fat-quarter selections than does one with a light background.

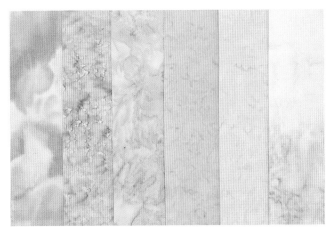
Background fabrics can inspire other fabric choices.

■ **A fabric collection:** You can take advantage of precoordinated fabrics in a collection or line, like my *Meow* fabrics. The motifs are designed to harmonize, the same dye colors are repeated, and the ultimate look when you combine them in backgrounds, borders, and other quilt elements is very together.

■ **A color:** Do you (or the quilt's young recipient) have a favorite color? Have the parents chosen a color for their baby's room that you'd like to match or coordinate with? Or perhaps there's a color you've never worked with but are eager to try. Use this color—in all its variations—as your inspiration. Don't be afraid to think outside the pink-and-blue box if you feel so inclined. For example, in my quilt *Good Luck Pets* (page 32), I used Japanese fabrics in a classic indigo color, enlivened with charming bunnies, kittens, and owls. Barbara Dau chose fabric with a black background, sprinkled with pastel motifs, for her *Lollipops* (page 26). And, of course, children of all ages love bright, zingy colors.

A color—in all its variations and values—can be a great jumping-off point.

Once you have a starting point, you are ready to choose the fat quarters and other fabrics for your quilt. As a rule, a variety of *colors*, *values*, and *prints* will make your quilt more interesting. You work with color every day. However, value and print may be new terms to you.

■ **Value** simply refers to how light or dark a fabric appears when placed next to its neighbors. Value creates contrast and allows you to see the pattern emerge. Even if you make a one-color (monochromatic) quilt like Susie Kincy's *Beautiful Blossoms* (page 27), the range of values within that single color is what makes the quilt work.

■ **Print** refers to the pattern on the fabric—stripes, airplanes, kittens, polka dots, and so on. Prints can be large-, medium-, or small-scale. Small-scale prints often have a delicate charm; large-scale prints can be bolder and more dramatic and are a fun choice for children's quilts. The fish motif fabric in Carla Zimmerman's *Wishing Fishies* (page 26) is a great example of a large-scale print, while the fabrics in my *Nursery Medley* (page 57) have small-scale charm. Some fabrics are *directional*, such as the fabric in Cheryl Gilman's *Dashing through the Snow* (page 49). If you use directional fabrics, be sure to read the special cutting notes with the individual quilt patterns.

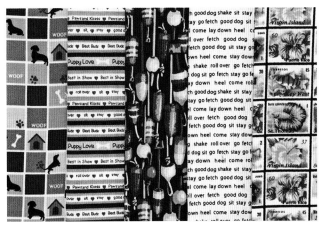
Examples of directional fabric

I like to mix it up, as I did in my *Spring View Embroidery* quilt (page 19) with my *Spring View* fabric collection. I designed a small-scale blender fabric, a larger-scale print, a subtle tone-on-tone print, and a print that continues the theme.

Stripes are always fun! A mixture of textures, layers of color, and a bold departure from your comfort zone make for a great fat-quarter quilt. For more information on using color, see my book *Get Creative! with M'Liss Rae Hawley*, available from C&T Publishing (see Resources, page 86).

Aim for a variety of prints (pattern and scale) and values in your fabric selection.

COLOR SELECTION CONFIDENCE

If you are unsure what color combinations to use or if you just need a little help breaking out of your color comfort zone, try using a portable tool, such as the 3-in-1 Color Tool, available from C&T Publishing (see Resources, page 86). These tools are especially helpful when choosing a shade from one color family. You can also use a classic color wheel, which illustrates the twelve pure colors and the relationships among them. I often use the color wheel as an additional guideline for choosing the color schemes for my quilts.

CHOOSING BACKGROUND FABRIC

How important is the background fabric? It is as significant as your fat quarters! The background fabric may represent up to half of the pieced quilt. Choosing a background fabric may not be the first decision you make, but then again you may have a wonderful piece of background fabric you want to build your quilt around.

Each pattern in this book uses a single background fabric for a simple, fresh look, which is especially appropriate in these smaller quilts. Background fabrics are often relatively light in value, creating a nice contrast with foreground fat-quarter fabrics. Of course, this is not an absolute! Assess your fat-quarter assortment. Depending on what you see, you may prefer to go darker for your background for a different look.

Examples of assorted light background fabrics

Quilters often choose neutral colors for backgrounds. Technically, neutral means free from color (examples of neutral colors are white, gray, and black), but I like to think that quilters can take liberties and add their own personal neutral colors to the standard list. Your neutral may simply be your favorite color—be it yellow or red—in its lightest value.

As always, you can take your cue from the theme, or focus, fabric. Is the lightest value white or beige? In my *Adrienne's Magic Wand* quilt (page 38), I used a light-colored background with "love" written on it. My *Best Friends* quilt (page 50) has a background of dog motifs on beige fabric, which carries out the canine theme. Does the theme fabric lend itself to a colored background—your favorite neutral? Finding the right background fabric or fabrics for your fat-quarter quilt is just another step in a wonderful journey. Take time in making choices now. The end results will be well worth it.

Examples of background fabrics and their companion focus fabrics

CHOOSING BORDER FABRICS

Most of the quilt patterns in this book include a narrow inner border between the center quilt design and the outer, wider border. You'll want to choose border fabrics that complement and enhance your design, rather than overpower it.

Many prepackaged fat-quarter packets are cut from fabrics that have just arrived at your local quilt shop. As a result, the fabrics in the packet are usually still available on the bolt. Repeating one of the fat quarters as your border fabric is a can't-miss method for finishing your quilt.

Large-scale prints make great borders for fat-quarter quilts. You'll need to plan ahead, though. Some large-scale prints are pictorial, directional, or both, as in my *Giddy Up!* quilt (page 54), so they may require extra yardage, as well as extra time and effort in the planning and cutting.

Examples of large-scale border fabrics

There are many other options for selecting an appropriate border fabric:

■ If your quilt features a wide range of prints, colors, or both, a multicolored novelty print or fantasy floral can tie them together. Annette Barca's *Bugs A-Buzzing* (page 43) and Lucia Pan's *Rose Garden* (page 61) are good examples.

■ A border fabric chosen to reflect the quilt's theme can't miss. John James's *School Daze* (page 49) demonstrates the success of a theme-inspired border.

■ Sometimes a border fabric that repeats a color in the background fabric can really pick up a quilt. A good example is Clara Hagglund's *Buzzin', Around* (page 56), which has a striking inner border of light green that echoes the dragonflies' wings.

Now that you've gotten started, no doubt you'll come up with many of your own creative solutions.

CHOOSING BINDING AND BACKING FABRIC

Usually the binding is the darkest fabric in the quilt, or it repeats the fabric in the outer border. I like to continue the motif or theme of the outer border in my choice of binding fabric. If, for instance, I use a floral print in the outer border, I'll use the same print or another, similar floral print as the binding, as I did in my *Spring View Embroidery* (page 19).

As for the backing, I always tell my students that the back of the quilt is as important as the front! Put some thought into choosing your backing fabric. Use a special fabric that relates to the fabrics on the quilt front and adds a touch of fun.

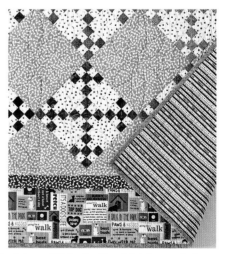
In *Best Friends* (page 50) the backing fabric is a perfect companion to the top.

tools and notions

You don't need a lot of fancy gadgets or special equipment to make a quilt. The basics, including a sewing machine in good working order and typical rotary-cutting supplies, work perfectly. Here is a list of what you'll need, with thoughts about my favorite features:

Rotary cutter: This cutting tool, similar to a pizza cutter, makes cutting fabric strips and pieces a breeze. Choose one with a reliable safety catch. The blade can get dull, so keep replacements on hand.

Cutting mat: This special cutting surface can stand up to sharp rotary blades without sustaining damage. I like the green, gridded variety; 18″ × 24″ is the most versatile size, for home and to take to class. Lines indicating 45° angles are helpful.

Acrylic rulers: These sturdy see-through rulers include all the essential measurements and increments. Try the 6″ × 24″ and 6″ × 12″ sizes, preferably with 45° angles indicated.

Ruler grips: These clear adhesive tabs stick to the bottom of your acrylic rulers to keep them from slipping as you cut.

Pins: My favorites are fine glass-head silk pins, because they don't leave unsightly holes in the fabric.

Scissors: You'll need both fabric scissors and small embroidery-type scissors for cutting thread.

Seam ripper: Believe it or not, this is my favorite notion! (Even the most experienced quilter makes mistakes.) This allows you to cut the stitches in a misplaced seam easily. Choose one with an ergonomic handle.

Thread: Select 100% cotton thread in a neutral color for piecing—both on top and in the bobbin. For hand quilting, choose 100% cotton thread. Cotton, rayon, polyester, monofilament, or other specialty threads designed for machine quilting are available to the machine quilter (see Threads, page 81).

Sewing machine needles: Keep a good supply on hand to change after each project.

Sewing machine: Any sewing machine that sews a straight, even stitch will work just fine for piecing quilts. Use a ¼″ presser foot, called a quilter's foot, to help keep your piecing accurate. If your machine did not come with this foot, I strongly recommend that you buy one!

Additional attachments: A dual-feed, or walking, foot is a must for straight-line quilting and for applying binding by machine. An open-toe stippling foot, also called a darning foot, is useful for free-motion quilting (see Quilting Your Quilt, pages 81–82).

Marking tool: To mark quilting designs on your quilt, choose a special marking tool, such as chalk, a water-soluble marker, or a silver pencil, available at quilting and fabric stores.

My handy Quilters and Crafters Value Kit, available from OLFA (see Resources, page 86), gives you a rotary cutter, 6″ × 12″ ruler, and cutting mat all in one package.

PROJECTS

baby's windows *quilt*

Alexander Takes Manhattan
**Designed and made by M'Liss Rae Hawley,
machine quilted by Barbara Dau, 2008.**

Finished quilt: 31½″ × 41½″
Finished block: 10″

In this quilt I feature the Muppets, which are beloved in my family. My son Alexander's first favorite movie was *The Muppet Movie*, which he loved to watch at home and at his grandparents' house, snuggled under his quilt.

Years later, I had the honor of visiting the Muppet Mansion in Manhattan, where I interviewed Cheryl Henson for *M'Liss's World of Quilts*, my PBS TV show. Afterward I wrote a letter on Muppet stationery to Alexander—by then a U.S. Marine serving in the Middle East—telling him about my visit. He was so excited!

So I embroidered the Muppets for this quilt with love and great memories. To set off the "windows," I chose colorful batiks and surrounded the blocks with a fun floral fabric that picks up the batik colors.

Have fun choosing your own favorite images for your version of this pattern!

materials

Fat quarters require 17½″ × 20″ of usable fabric. All other yardages are based on 40″-wide fabric.

- Fat quarters of 4 assorted fabrics
- ⅝ yard of light-value fabric for embroidered block centers
- ¼ yard of fabric for inner border
- ¾ yard of fabric for outer border
- ½ yard of fabric for binding
- 1½ yards of fabric for backing
- ⅓ yard of fabric for a hanging sleeve (optional)
- 40″ × 50″ piece of batting
- A favorite embroidery collection for embroidered block centers*
- 1¾ yard of 12″-wide stabilizer for embroideries

You'll need 6 motifs. (For Muppet embroideries information, see Resources, page 86.)

cutting

Cut along the 20″ length of the fat quarters. For the remaining fabrics, cut strips on the crosswise grain (from selvage to selvage).

From each of Fat Quarters 1 and 2:

Cut 4 strips, 3″ × 20″.

From each of Fat Quarters 3 and 4:

Cut 5 strips, 1¾″ × 20″.

From the light-value fabric:

Cut 2 strips, 9½″ × 40″; crosscut into 6 squares, 9½″ × 9½″.

From the inner border fabric:

Cut 4 strips, 1½″ × 40″.

From the outer border fabric:

Cut 4 strips, 5″ × 40″.

From the binding fabric:

Cut 5 strips, 3″ × 40″.

From the hanging sleeve fabric:

Cut 1 strip, 8½″ × 40″.

CREATIVE OPTIONS: TWO WAYS TO GO

I used my *Spring View* fabric collection for *Spring View Embroidery* and *Agatha & Friends* (pages 19 and 21). One version features the coordinating embroideries in the blocks. Check out the block with my dachshund, Agatha—I embroidered her on the fabric (page 21)! The other features fabrics in the blocks instead of embroideries. To "fussy cut" the fabric so the images will be nicely framed, carefully place a plastic template on the fabric to preview the motif before you cut. (Also see Plan Before Cut, page 24.)

CREATIVE OPTIONS: FINISH WITH THE FAT QUARTERS

You can use any leftover fabric from each fat quarter to make the binding for your quilt (see Making and Applying Binding, page 83) or to make a label that coordinates with the quilt front, as described in Creating a Label (page 85). Another idea is to use leftover fabric, plus some fabrics from your stash, to make a coordinating doll quilt of your own creation.

making the blocks

This finished quilt includes 6 blocks. The drawings show my Spring View embroideries, shown on page 19 (see Resources, page 86). For embroidery specifics, see Tips for Machine Embroidery (page 20).

1. Following the manufacturer's instructions, use the stabilizer to prepare each 9½" × 9½" square of light-value fabric for embroidery. Select an embroidery collection, and embroider a different motif in the center of each stabilized square. (Adjust the size of the 9½" × 9½" squares as needed to fit your embroidery hoop.)

2. Carefully remove the stabilizer, and press the finished embroidery right side down on a terry towel, then trim to 5½" × 5½". (Use a 5½"-square ruler or place tape on a larger ruler to measure off a 5½" square.) Don't worry about the grain of the fabric; cut the square to best suit the embroidery motif. Make 6.

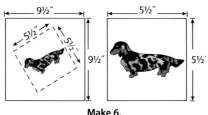

Make 6.

3. Sew a 3" × 20" strip from Fat Quarter 1 to a 3" × 20" strip from Fat Quarter 2, right sides together, along the long edges. Press toward the dark fabric. Repeat with the remaining strips, for a total of 4 strip sets, each 5½" × 20". Label these Set A.

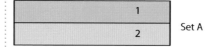

Set A

4. Crosscut the Set A strip sets into 24 segments, each 3" wide.

Set A

5. Sew a 1¾" × 20" strip from Fat Quarter 3 to a 1¾" × 20" strip from Fat Quarter 4, right sides together, along the long edges. Press toward the dark fabric. Repeat with the remaining strips, for a total of 5 strip sets, each 3" × 20". Label these Set B.

Set B

6. Crosscut the Set B strip sets into 48 segments, each 1¾" wide.

Set B

7. Arrange 2 segments from Step 6 as shown. Sew the segments together, carefully matching the center seams. Press. Make 24. Each unit should measure 3" × 3".

Make 24.

8. Arrange 1 of the 5½" × 5½" embroidered squares, 4 units from Step 4, and 4 units from Step 7, taking care to position them as shown.

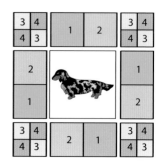

9. Sew the units together into horizontal rows. Press.

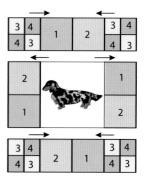

10. Sew the rows together, carefully matching the seams. Press. The block should measure 10½" × 10½". Make 6 blocks total.

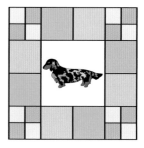

assembling the quilt

1. Arrange the blocks in 3 horizontal rows of 2 blocks each.

2. Sew the blocks into rows as shown in the assembly diagram (below). Press. Sew the rows together. Press.

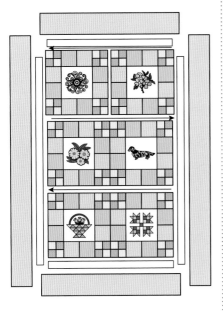

Assembly diagram

3. Refer to Adding Borders (page 79). Measure, trim, and sew the 1½"-wide inner borders to the top and bottom of the quilt. Press the seams toward the borders. Repeat to sew inner borders to the sides.

4. Repeat Step 3 to add the 5"-wide outer borders.

finishing the quilt

Refer to pages 79–85 for more detailed information on finishing your quilt.

1. Prepare the backing.

2. Layer the quilt top, batting, and backing; baste.

3. Hand or machine quilt as desired.

4. Piece together the 3"-wide strips you cut from your binding fabric or leftover fat quarters to bind the edges of the quilt.

5. Add a hanging sleeve and label if desired.

IN THE RIGHT DIRECTION

If your embroidery motif is directional, like my Muppet and Spring View images, be sure to plan its placement carefully!

Spring View Embroidery, 31½" × 41½", designed and made by M'Liss Rae Hawley, machine quilted by Barbara Dau, 2008.

■ Prewash the fabric you plan to use as background for the embroidery designs. Washing will preshrink the fabric, which is a necessary step.

■ Begin your embroidery with a new needle and change it during the process if the point becomes dull. Skipped stitches are one indication of a dull needle. Some embroidery designs have more than 10,000 stitches. A dull needle can distort the design.

■ Outfit your machine with an embroidery foot.

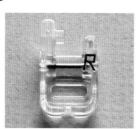

■ Prewind several bobbins with polyester, rayon, or cotton bobbin-fill thread. Or purchase prewound bobbins. Choose white or black, using the background fabric as your guide; or you may want to change the bobbin thread as the color of the top thread changes.

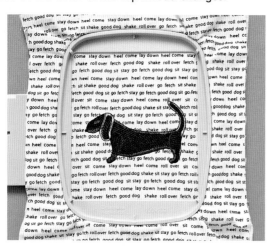

■ Use a fabric stabilizer under the background fabric to keep it from stretching. My favorite is a midweight tear-away product manufactured by Sulky (see Resources, page 86). I use it on 100% cotton fabric. Whichever you choose, read the manufacturer's instructions carefully. If the fabric is prone to puckering, try a water-soluble or heat-sensitive stabilizer.

■ When embroidering on flannel, choose a heavier-weight Sulky. If you are embroidering delicate design elements, such as stems, using a single running or outline stitch, use a water-soluble stabilizer like Sulky Solvy on the *top* to keep your stitches from sinking into the fabric's nap.

■ An embroidery hoop is key; it keeps the fabric from shifting as you embroider the designs. If possible, place the fabric in the hoop so that it is straight on the grain. Avoid puckers and pleats. The fabric should be pulled taut but not too tight.

■ Stitch a test of the desired embroidery design, using the fabric, threads, and stabilizer you plan to use for the project. You'll be able to tell whether the thread tension is correct, whether the thread coverage is sufficient, and whether the embroidered design will look good on the background fabric you've chosen so you can make any necessary adjustments. If you wish, you can incorporate your test design into your label or quilt backing.

Detail of *Spring View Embroidery*

Detail of *Agatha & Friends*

Detail of *Crib Critters*

Agatha & Friends, 31½″ × 41½″,
designed and made by M'Liss Rae Hawley,
machine quilted by Barbara Dau, 2008.

Crib Critters, 30¼″ × 39¾″,
made by John James,
machine quilted by Barbara Dau, 2008.

Detail of *Frogs and Friends*

Detail of *Curious George Discovers Quilts*

Frogs and Friends, 30⅞″ × 40½″,
made and machine quilted by Clara Hagglund, 2008.

Curious George Discovers Quilts, 32″ × 41″,
made by Susie Kincy,
machine quilted by Barbara Dau, 2008.

building blocks *quilt*

I Love Kitties!
Designed and made by M'Liss Rae Hawley,
machine quilted by Barbara Dau, 2008.

Finished quilt: 47″ × 58¾″
Finished block: 10½″

Building Blocks gives you a great opportunity to showcase a fabric collection. When you choose a themed fabric, especially one from a collection like my *Meow* fabrics, your quilt will just naturally look pulled-together. (My four cats—Garfield, Clairabelle, and especially Bridge and Fiona, the calico sisters—inspired this collection.) The simple framed squares in this quilt pattern give you an opportunity to display large-scale prints or directional fabrics, as well as to play with mixing fabrics with related motifs.

You're sure to have plenty of fun when you play with "building" a quilt from big blocks of fabric!

materials

Fat quarters require 17½″ × 20″ of usable fabric. All other yardages are based on 40″-wide fabric.

- ■ Fat quarters of 4 assorted fabrics
- ■ 1 yard of fabric for block sashing and cornerstones
- ■ ⅝ yard of fabric for lattice
- ■ 1 yard of fabric for outer border*
- ■ ⅝ yard of fabric for binding
- ■ 3⅞ yards of fabric for backing
- ■ ½ yard of fabric for a hanging sleeve (optional)
- ■ 55″ × 67″ piece of batting

Allow extra for directional fabric.

cutting

Cut along the 20″ length of the fat quarters (except for the 7½″ squares). For the remaining fabrics, cut strips on the crosswise grain (from selvage to selvage).

From each fat quarter:

Cut 3 squares, 7½″ × 7½″.

From the block sashing and cornerstones fabric:

For the sashing, cut 12 strips, 2¼″ × 40″; crosscut each into 2 strips, 2¼″ × 11″, and 2 strips, 2¼″ × 7½″ (a total of 24 each).

For the cornerstones, cut 1 strip, 1¾″ × 40″; crosscut into 20 squares, 1¾″ × 1¾″.

From the lattice fabric:

Cut 11 strips, 1¾″ × 40″; crosscut into 31 strips, 1¾″ × 11″.

From the border fabric:

Cut 5 strips, 5½″ × 40″.

From the binding fabric:

Cut 6 strips, 3″ × 40″.

From the hanging sleeve fabric:

Cut 2 strips, 8½″ × 40″.

✻ PLAN BEFORE YOU CUT

Cut a 7½″ × 7½″ square of clear template plastic. (Look for it at your local fabric store.) Mark the ¼″ seamlines and place it on your fabric. Move it around until it frames the most pleasing "picture" of the fabric's motif, and make that the center of your block.

✻ CREATIVE OPTIONS: FINISH WITH THE FAT QUARTERS

You can use any leftover fabric from each fat quarter to make the binding for your quilt (see Making and Applying Binding, page 83), or to make a label that coordinates with the quilt front, as described in Creating a Label (page 85). Another idea is to use leftover fabric, plus some fabrics from your stash, to make a coordinating doll quilt of your own creation.

---

making the blocks

This finished quilt includes 12 blocks, 3 of each fat quarter.

1. Sew 2¼″ × 7½″ sashing strips to the top and bottom of each 7½″ × 7½″ square. Press toward the sashing strips.

2. Sew 2¼″ × 11″ sashing strips to both sides of each square. Press toward the sides. Square up each block to 11″ × 11″.

assembling the quilt

1. Lay out the blocks in a pleasing arrangement of fat-quarter fabrics, in 4 horizontal rows of 3 blocks each, as shown in the assembly diagram (right). Sew 4 lattice strips, 1¾″ × 11″, and 3 blocks together, alternating the blocks and strips to make a block row, as shown; press toward the lattice strips. Make 4 rows.

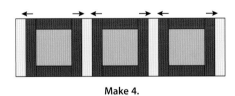

Make 4.

2. Sew 3 lattice strips, 1¾″ × 11″, and 4 cornerstones, 1¾″ × 1¾″, together, alternating them to make a lattice row, as shown; press toward the lattice strips. Make 5 rows.

Make 5.

3. Lay out the block rows and lattice rows, alternating them as shown in the assembly diagram. Sew the rows together; press.

Assembly diagram

4. Refer to Adding Borders (page 79). Measure, fit, and sew the 5½″-wide border strips to the top and bottom of the quilt. Press the seams toward the borders. Repeat to sew borders to the sides of the quilt.

finishing the quilt

Refer to pages 79–85 for more detailed information on finishing your quilt.

1. Prepare the backing.

2. Layer the quilt top, batting, and backing; baste.

3. Hand or machine quilt as desired.

4. Piece together the 3″-wide strips you cut from the binding fabric or leftover fat quarters to bind the edges of the quilt.

5. Add a hanging sleeve and label if desired.

Detail of *Lollipops*

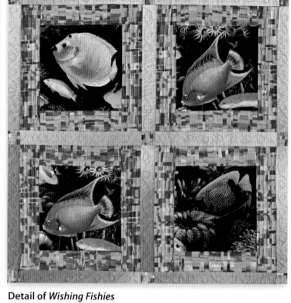

Detail of *Wishing Fishies*

Lollipops, 45″ × 56″,
made and machine quilted by Barbara Dau, 2008

Wishing Fishies, 46½″ × 60½″,
made by Carla Zimmerman,
machine quilted by Barbara Dau, 2008

Detail of *Beautiful Blossoms*

Detail of *Dance Baby Dance*

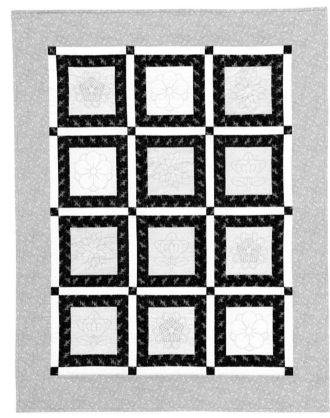

Beautiful Blossoms, 47″ × 58″,
made and machine quilted by Susie Kincy, 2008

Dance Baby Dance, 46″ × 59″,
made by Anastasia Riordan,
machine quilted by Barbara Dau, 2008

It's a Girl!
Designed, made, and machine quilted
by M'Liss Rae Hawley, 2008.

Finished quilt: 35¼″ × 47″
Finished block: 10½″

FAST, FAT QUARTER BABY QUILTS WITH M'LISS RAE HAWLEY

Building Blocks is such a versatile pattern that you can easily create a smaller, six-block version to make a crib quilt. For this version, I used my signature black and white—plus brights—color combination to make a baby quilt that's different and fun. This combination is known to be highly visible and attractive to newborns and young babies, so it's the perfect choice! A six-block quilt also makes an appealing wallhanging for a baby's or child's room.

materials

Fat quarters require 17½" × 20" of usable fabric. All other yardages are based on 40"-wide fabric.

- ■ Fat quarters of 3 assorted fabrics
- ■ ⅝ yard of fabric for block sashing and cornerstones
- ■ ⅜ yard of fabric for lattice
- ■ ⅞ yard of fabric for outer border*
- ■ ½ yard of fabric for binding
- ■ 3¼ yards of fabric for backing
- ■ ⅓ yard of fabric for a hanging sleeve (optional)
- ■ 43" × 55" piece of batting

Allow extra for directional fabric.

cutting

From each fat quarter:

Cut 2 squares, 7½" × 7½".

From the block sashing and cornerstones fabric:

For the sashing, cut 6 strips, 2¼" × 40"; crosscut each into 2 strips, 2¼" × 11", and 2 strips, 2¼" × 7½" (for a total of 12 each).

For the cornerstones, cut 1 strip, 1¾" × 40"; crosscut into 12 squares, 1¾" × 1¾".

From the lattice fabric:

Cut 6 strips, 1¾" × 40"; crosscut into 17 strips, 1¾" × 11".

From the border fabric:

Cut 4 strips, 5½" × 40".

From the binding fabric:

Cut 5 strips, 3" × 40".

From the hanging sleeve fabric:

Cut 1 strip, 8½" × 40".

making the quilt

1. Follow the instructions in Making the Blocks for the larger quilt (page 25). Make 6 blocks, 2 of each fat quarter.

2. Arrange and assemble the blocks as described for the larger quilt in Assembling the Quilt (page 25). Sew 3 lattice strips, 1¾" × 11", and 2 blocks together, alternating the blocks and strips to make 3 block rows.

3. Sew lattice strips, 1¾" × 11", and 3 cornerstones, 1¾" × 1¾" together, alternating them to make a lattice row; press. Make 4 rows. Lay out the block rows and lattice rows, alternating them as shown in the assembly diagram (below). Press the rows in opposite directions. Sew the rows together. Press.

4. Refer to Adding Borders (page 79) to measure, fit, and sew the 5½"-wide border strips to the top and bottom of the quilt. Press the seams toward the borders. Repeat to sew borders to the sides of the quilt.

5. Finish the quilt as described for the larger quilt in Finishing the Quilt (page 25).

Assembly diagram

MITERED CORNERS

When I made this quilt, I decided that the border fabric looked better with mitered corners. If you would like to miter your borders, refer to my book *Round Robin Renaissance*, available from C&T Publishing (see Resources, page 86).

Detail of Soft and Cuddly

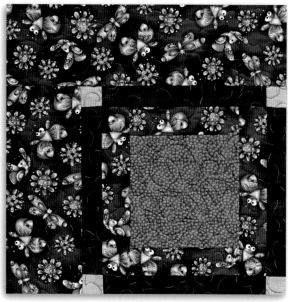

Detail of Butterflies, Dragonflies & Bumblebees, Oh My!

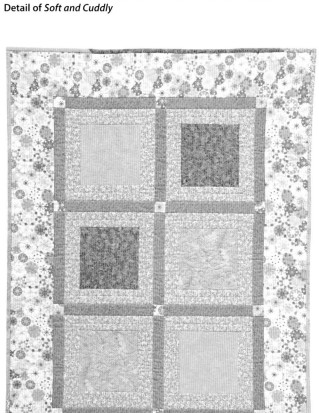

Soft and Cuddly, 35¼˝ × 47˝,
made and machine quilted by Vicki DeGraaf, 2008

Butterflies, Dragonflies & Bumblebees, Oh My! 35½˝ × 47˝,
made by Peggy Johnson,
machine quilted by Stacie Johnson, 2008

FAST, FAT QUARTER BABY QUILTS WITH M'LISS RAE HAWLEY

Childhood, 45″ × 34¼″,
made by John James,
machine quilted by Barbara Dau, 2008.

Detail of *Childhood*

A SPECIAL VERSION

Building Blocks is so versatile that you can make a six-block version with a horizontal layout, like John James's *Childhood*, made to feature charming larger-size Hummel embroideries.

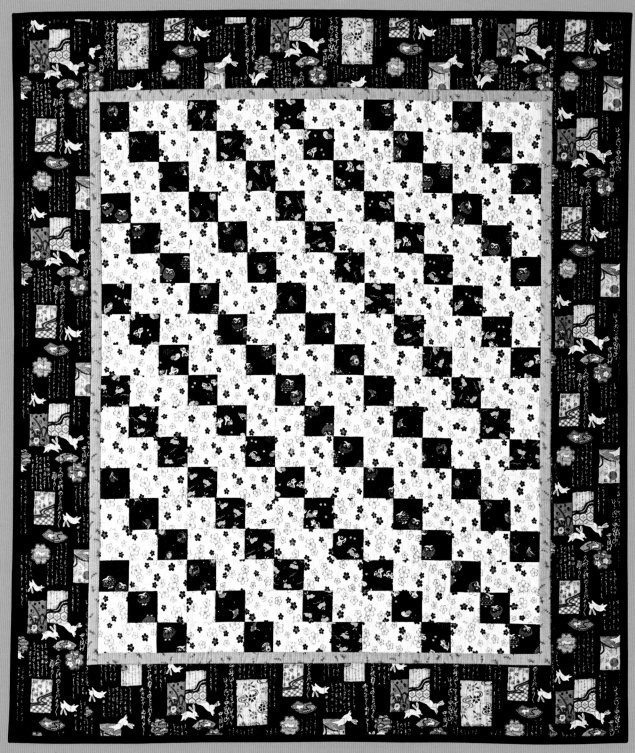

Good Luck Pets
**Designed and made by M'Liss Rae Hawley,
machine quilted by Barbara Dau, 2008.**

Finished quilt: 42″ × 48″
Finished block: 6″

I called this pattern *First Steps* because the diagonal runs of little squares remind me of the way a toddler takes those first small steps across the floor. The pattern is also a perfect first step into quilting for a beginner, because it's so quick and easy to make. Small-scale motifs like the miniature bunnies, kittens, and owls in the Japanese fabrics I used have that special whimsy that's just right for a baby quilt.

The background makes its own statement in this pattern, so opt for a fabric with contrasting color and an interesting motif. I chose a light beige Japanese fabric sprinkled with dainty flowers.

You're going to enjoy making this quilt so much that you'll want to create one for every baby in your life!

materials

Fat quarters require 17½" × 20" of usable fabric. All other yardages are based on 40"-wide fabric.

▥ Fat quarters of 4 assorted fabrics

▥ 1 yard of fabric for background

▥ ¼ yard of fabric for inner border

▥ 1 yard of fabric for outer border

▥ ⅝ yard of fabric for binding*

▥ 3¼ yards of fabric for backing

▥ ½ yard of fabric for a hanging sleeve (optional)

▥ 50" × 56" piece of batting

Or use the extra 10" from each fat quarter.

cutting

Cut along the 20" length of the fat quarters. If the motif on your fat-quarter fabric is directional, you may want to cut along the 17½" straight of grain.

For the remaining fabrics, cut strips on the crosswise grain (from selvage to selvage).

From each fat quarter:

Cut 3 strips, 2½" × 20".*

If any of your fat quarters has less than 20" of usable fabric, you'll need to cut an additional strip. For fabric with a directional motif, cut an additional strip along the 17½" straight of grain.

From the background fabric:

Cut 4 strips, 4½" × 40"; crosscut into 8 strips, 4½" × 20".*

Cut 4 strips, 2½" × 40"; crosscut into 8 strips, 2½" × 20".*

If you don't have 40" of usable fabric, or if you needed additional fat-quarter strips, you'll need to cut additional background-fabric strips.

From the inner border fabric:

Cut 4 strips, 1¼" × 40".

From the outer border fabric:

Cut 5 strips, 5½" × 40".

From the binding fabric:

If using yardage, cut 6 strips, 3" × 40".

If using extra fat-quarter fabric, cut 3 strips, 3" × 20", from each fat quarter.

From the hanging sleeve fabric:

Cut 2 strips, 8½" × 40".

CREATIVE OPTIONS: FINISH WITH THE FAT QUARTERS

You can use the extra 10 inches from each fat quarter to make the binding for your quilt (see Making and Applying Binding, page 83), or to make a label that coordinates with the quilt front as described in Creating a Label (page 85). Another idea is to use leftover fabric, plus some fabrics from your stash, to make a coordinating doll quilt of your own creation.

STAY ORGANIZED

Stack together strips and units of matching fat-quarter fabrics as you cut them. Label them 1, 2, 3, and 4.

making the blocks

This finished quilt includes 30 blocks, 8 from each fat quarter (you'll have 2 left over).

1. Sew 1 of the 2½" × 20" strips from Fat Quarter 1 to 1 of the 4½" × 20" background strips along a long edge. Make 1 more matching strip set. Press toward the fat-quarter strip. Repeat with strips from Fat Quarters 2, 3, and 4, for a total of 8 strip sets. Label these Set A.

2. Crosscut a total of 16 segments, each 2½" wide, from the Fat Quarter 1 strip sets labeled Set A. Repeat for the Fat Quarter 2, 3, and 4, strip sets for a grand total of 64 segments.

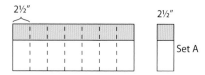

Cut 8 segments from each fat quarter Set A.

3. Sew the remaining 2½" × 20" strip from Fat Quarter 1 between 2 of the 2½" × 20" background strips, as shown below, along the long edges. Press toward the fat-quarter fabric. Repeat with strips from Fat Quarters 2, 3, and 4, for a total of 4 strip sets. Label these Set B.

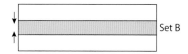

4. Crosscut 8 segments, each 2½" wide, from each Set B strip set for a total of 32 segments.

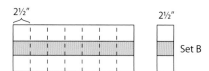

Cut 8 segments from each fat quarter Set B.

5. To make a block, select 2 Set A segments from Fat Quarter 1 and 1 Set B segment from Fat Quarter 1. Sew the units together as shown below.

6. Make 8 blocks of each fat-quarter fabric. Press.

Note:

You will have 2 blocks left over. If you wish, you may use them for the label on the back of your quilt (see Creating a Label, page 85).

assembling the quilt

1. Lay out the blocks in 6 horizontal rows of 5 blocks each, as shown in the assembly diagram, so that blocks of matching fat quarters form diagonal chains.

2. Sew the blocks into 6 horizontal rows. Press the rows in opposite directions. Sew the rows together, carefully matching the seams. Press.

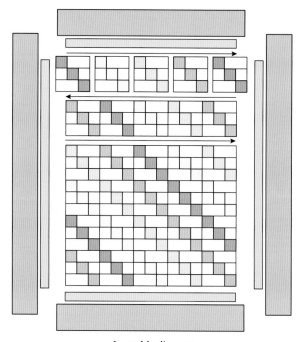

Assembly diagram

FAST, FAT QUARTER BABY QUILTS WITH M'LISS RAE HAWLEY

3. Refer to Adding Borders (page 79) to measure, fit, and sew 1¼″-wide inner border strips to the top and bottom of the quilt. Press the seams toward the borders. Repeat to sew inner borders to the sides of the quilt.

4. Repeat Step 3 to measure, trim, and sew the 5½″-wide outer borders to the quilt.

CREATIVE OPTIONS—CHECK OUT THE BACK!

For the quilt backing, I continued my Japanese fabric theme with a Noren fabric panel, *Owls on Tree*. I sewed it to the quilt backing, along with my labels, before it was quilted. The machine quilting shows up beautifully on the back.

finishing the quilt

Refer to pages 79–85 for more detailed information on finishing your quilt.

1. Prepare the backing.

2. Layer the quilt top, batting, and backing; baste.

3. Hand or machine quilt as desired.

4. Piece together the 3″-wide strips you cut from the binding fabric or leftover fat quarters to bind the edges of the quilt.

5. Add a hanging sleeve and label if desired.

Detail of *For the Little Fireman*

For the Little Fireman, 41½″ × 47½″, made by Carla Zimmerman, machine quilted by Arlene Anderson, 2008.

Detail of *Tea Party*

Detail of *Lullaby Stairway*

Tea Party, 41″ × 48″,
made by Susie Kincy,
machine quilted by Barbara Dau, 2008.

Lullaby Stairway, 38″ × 45″,
made by Anastasia Riordan,
machine quilted by Barbara Dau, 2008.

Detail of *Resting on the Misty Seas*

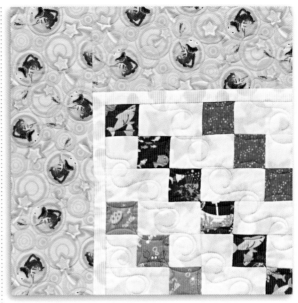

Detail of *Kermit Visits the Aquarium*

Resting on the Misty Seas, 42″ × 48″,
made by Vicki DeGraaf,
machine quilted by Doris Ellis, 2008.

Kermit Visits the Aquarium, 41″ × 47″,
made by Annette Barca,
machine quilted by Barbara Dau, 2008.

motion commotion

quilt

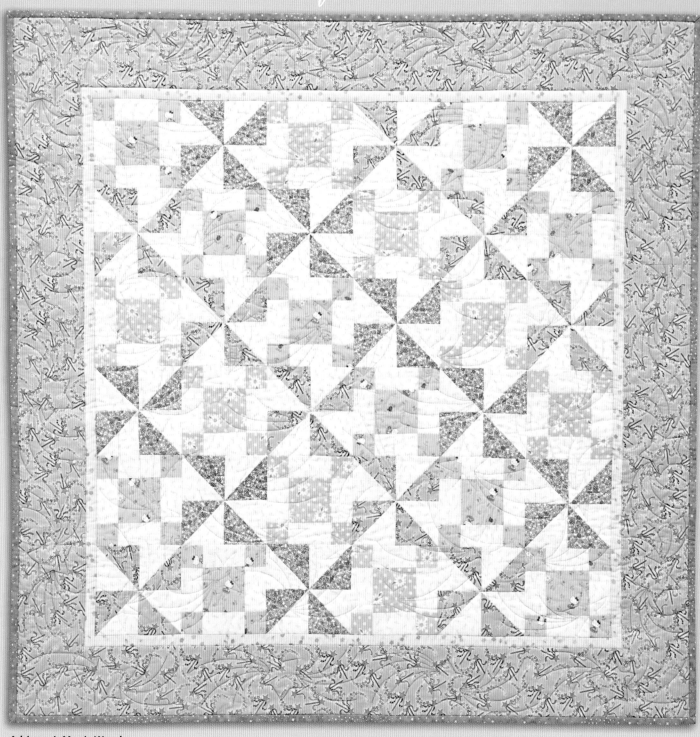

Adrienne's Magic Wand
Designed and made by M'Liss Rae Hawley,
machine quilted by Barbara Dau, 2008.

 Finished quilt: 47" × 47"
Finished block: 6"

 Doll Quilt on page 41

I originally designed this block combination as *Spinning My Wheels*, for my book *Make Your First Quilt With M'Liss Rae Hawley*, available from C&T Publishing (see Resources, page 86). It's such a fun effect that I couldn't resist including it in this book. I've adapted it to make use of four different fat-quarter fabrics. The result is a design that's as lively and full of action as a crawling baby or a busy toddler! You'll find that wonderful secondary patterns emerge depending on the colors, values, and scale of the fabrics you choose.

My 23-year-old daughter, Adrienne, picked out the fabric for this quilt. She's been my shopping partner since she was born, and we have so many happy memories of buying fabric together, all over the world. (Well, at least she's been very patient!)

With this project, I offer a special bonus—a matching doll quilt! This small-size quilt makes a cute companion gift for a new baby or a thoughtful gift for his or her sibling. It's also a creative way to use the four extra blocks and leftover fabric from the full-size quilt. For guidance, see Make a Matching Doll Quilt! (page 41).

PERFECT SQUARES

Because the Pinwheel and Nine-Patch Variation blocks in this quilt are directly adjacent to each other, without intervening blocks, it's important to make sure your blocks are perfect 6½" squares. Follow my advice under Piecing (page 75) and Squaring the Blocks (page 77) to help you get it right.

---

materials

Fat quarters require 17½" × 20" of usable fabric. All other yardages are based on 40"-wide fabric.

▩ Fat quarters of 4 assorted fabrics

▩ 1⅛ yards of fabric for background

▩ ¼ yard of fabric for inner border

▩ ⅞ yard of fabric for outer border*

▩ ⅝ yard of fabric for binding

▩ 3¼ yards of fabric for backing

▩ ½ yard of fabric for a hanging sleeve (optional)

▩ 55" × 55" piece of batting

* Directional fabric will require more yardage.

 To make a matching doll quilt, buy an additional ⅔ yard of backing fabric.

To make a matching doll quilt, buy a 22" × 22" piece of diaper flannel.

cutting

Cut along the 20" length of the fat quarters. For the remaining fabrics, cut strips on the crosswise grain (from selvage to selvage).

From each of Fat Quarters 1 and 2:

Cut 4 strips, 3⅞" × 20"; crosscut into 20 squares, 3⅞" × 3⅞". Cut each square in half once diagonally to make 2 half-square triangles (40 total per fat quarter).

From each of Fat Quarters 3 and 4:

Cut 2 strips, 3½" × 20".

Cut 4 strips, 2" × 20".

From the background fabric:

Cut 4 strips, 3⅞" × 40"; crosscut into 40 squares, 3⅞" × 3⅞". Cut each square in half once diagonally to make 2 half-square triangles (80 total).

Cut 4 strips, 2" × 40"; crosscut into 2 pieces, 2" × 20", for the center section (8 total).

Cut 2 strips, 3½" × 40"; cut each into 2 strips, 20" long, for the top and bottom (4 total).

From the inner border fabric:

Cut 4 strips, 1¼" × 40".

From the outer border fabric:

Cut 5 strips, 5" × 40".

From the binding fabric:

Cut 6 strips, 3" × 40".

From the hanging sleeve fabric:

Cut 2 strips, 8½" × 40".

STAY ORGANIZED

Stack together strips and units of matching fat-quarter fabrics as you cut them. Label them 1, 2, 3, and 4.

---

assembling the blocks

This finished quilt includes 36 blocks. Make 10 blocks per fat quarter (you'll have 4 left over).

PINWHEEL BLOCKS

1. Sew a Fat Quarter 1 half-square triangle and a background half-square triangle together. Press toward the fat-quarter fabric. Make 40. Each unit should measure 3½″ × 3½″. Repeat for Fat Quarter 2.

Make 40.

2. Arrange 4 Fat Quarter 1 units from Step 1, taking care to rotate them as shown. Sew the units together into pairs. Press the pairs in opposite directions. Sew the pairs together, carefully matching the center seam. See Piecing Perfect Points the Easy Way (page 76) for guidance in matching points. Press. Make 10. Each block should measure 6½″ × 6½″. Repeat for Fat Quarter 2.

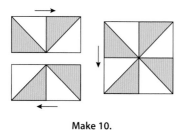

Make 10.

NINE-PATCH VARIATION BLOCKS

1. Sew a 3½″ × 20″ background strip between 2 of the 2″ × 20″ Fat Quarter 3 strips. Press toward the fat-quarter fabric. Make 2. Crosscut into 20 segments, 2″ × 6½″. Repeat for Fat Quarter 4.

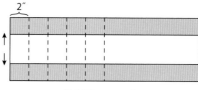

Cut 20 segments.

2. Sew a 3½″ × 20″ strip from Fat Quarter 3 between 2 of the 2″ × 20″ background strips. Press toward the fat-quarter fabric. Make 2. Crosscut each strip set into 5 segments, 3½″ × 6½″, for a total of 10 segments. Repeat for Fat Quarter 4.

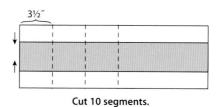

Cut 10 segments.

3. Sew Fat Quarter 3 segments from Step 1 to the top and bottom of each Fat Quarter 3 segment from Step 2, carefully matching the seams. Press. This block should measure 6½″ × 6½″. Make 10.

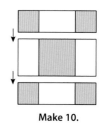

Make 10.

4. Repeat Step 3 with Fat Quarter 4 segments. Press. Each block should measure 6½″ × 6½″. Make 10.

assembling the quilt

1. Arrange the blocks in 6 horizontal rows of 6 blocks each as shown in the assembly diagram. You'll have 4 left over.

2. Sew the blocks into rows. Press the rows in opposite directions. Sew the rows together. Press.

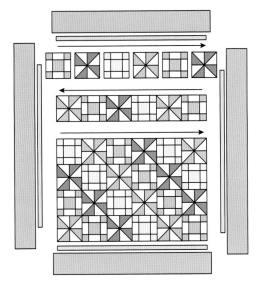

Assembly diagram

3. Refer to Adding Borders (page 79). Measure, trim, and sew the 1¼"-wide inner borders to the top and bottom of the quilt. Press the seams toward the borders. Repeat to sew the inner borders to the sides.

4. Repeat Step 3 to add the 5"-wide outer borders.

finishing the quilt

Refer to pages 79–85 for more detailed information on finishing your quilt.

1. Prepare the backing.

2. Layer the quilt top, batting, and backing; baste.

3. Hand or machine quilt as desired.

4. Piece together the 3"-wide strips you cut from the binding fabric to bind the edges of the quilt.

5. Add a hanging sleeve and label if desired.

MAKE A MATCHING DOLL QUILT!

Use the 4 leftover blocks you've already made to create a smaller, doll-size version of *Motion Commotion.*

■ Sew the 4 blocks together to make a $12^{1}/_{2}$″ × $12^{1}/_{2}$″ square.

■ Use fabrics left over from the quilt or new fabrics (purchased or from your stash) to make the inner and outer borders and binding:

From the inner border fabric, cut 2 strips, 1″ wide.

From the outer border fabric, cut 2 strips, 3″ wide.

From the binding fabric, cut 2 strips, $2^{7}/_{8}$″ wide.

■ Construct the borders, backing, and binding as described for the full-size quilt. The finished doll quilt will measure $18^{1}/_{2}$″ × $18^{1}/_{2}$″.

Adrienne's Magic Wand Doll Quilt, 18½″ × 18½″, **designed, made, and machine quilted by M'Liss Rae Hawley, 2008.**

Baby Bears Outside Doll Quilt, 18″ × 18″,
made and machine quilted by Susie Kincy, 2008.

Let's Play Outside, 47″ × 47″,
made by Susie Kincy,
machine quilted by Barbara Dau, 2008.

Gecko in Motion Doll Quilt, 19½″ × 19½″,
made and machine quilted by Barbara Dau, 2008.

Gecko in Motion, 46″ × 46″,
made and machine quilted by Barbara Dau, 2008.

Mini Wheels Doll Quilt, 18¼˝ × 18¼˝,
made and machine quilted by John James, 2008.

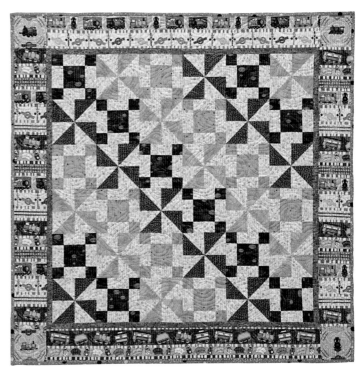

The Wheels on the Train Go Round and Round, 46˝ × 46˝,
made by John James,
machine quilted by Barbara Dau, 2008.

Bright-Colored Bugs Doll Quilt, 18˝ × 18˝,
made and machine quilted by Annette Barca, 2008.

Bugs A-Buzzing, 47˝ × 47˝,
made by Annette Barca,
machine quilted by Barbara Dau, 2008.

opportunity *quilt*

Playing in the Pumpkin Patch
Designed by M'Liss Rae Hawley,
machine quilted by Barbara Dau, 2008.

 Finished quilt: 54" × 62"

FAST, FAT QUARTER BABY QUILTS WITH M'LISS RAE HAWLEY

I designed the *Opportunity Quilt* pattern to give you an "opportunity" to use a large-scale print you love in a quilt that's fast and fun to make. I used my *Autumn View* fabric, featuring our family's orchard property and two of our pets, Calie and Matilda. Because it's so easy, you and your friends can also take the opportunity to get together and make this quilt for your favorite charity.

Your large-scale print (the focus fabric) has a finished height of 8 inches. I allowed an extra ¼ yard for possible fussy cutting (cutting the fabric so the motif, such as the pets, flowers, and moons in my fabric, will be placed in a certain way). Open your fabric and look at the piece as a whole before you cut the sections. Stagger the repeat images in the print when you cut the four sections, so that the images don't line up vertically on your finished quilt. This will give the quilt more variety and interest.

THE BIG PICTURE

Take the time to make sure those delightful animal and human figures in your large-scale prints don't wind up headless or armless! Vicki DeGraaf was careful to cut her fabric, which features children at play, so that all of the children's images are complete. For a full view of her *School Fun*, see page 48.

materials

Fat quarters require 17½" × 20" of usable fabric. All other yardages are based on 40"-wide fabric.

▦ ⅝ yard of light-value fabric or 3 fat quarters for checkerboards

▦ 3 fat quarters of dark-value fabric for checkerboards

▦ 1¼ yards of large-scale print focus fabric*

▦ ½ yard of fabric for inner border

▦ 1¼ yards of fabric for outer border

▦ ⅔ yard of fabric for binding

▦ 4 yards of fabric for backing

▦ ½ yard of fabric for a hanging sleeve (optional)

▦ 62" × 70" piece of batting

If you want to use 4 different focus fabrics, you will need ⅓ yard of each. School Daze by John James (page 49) is a lively example of this approach.

CREATIVE OPTIONS: FINISH WITH THE FAT QUARTERS

You can use any leftover fabric from each fat quarter to make the binding for your quilt (see Making and Applying Binding, page 83), or to make a label that coordinates with the quilt front as described in Creating a Label (page 85). Another idea is to use leftover fabric, plus some fabrics from your stash, to make a coordinating doll quilt of your own creation.

cutting

From the large-scale print focus fabric:

Cut 4 strips, 8½" × 40".

From the light checkerboard fabric:

Cut 9 strips, 2" × 40"; crosscut to make 18 strips, 2" × 20".

From each fat quarter of dark checkerboard fabric:

Cut 6 strips, 2" × 20".

From the inner border fabric:

Cut 5 strips, 2½" × 40".

From the outer border fabric:

Cut 6 strips, 6½" × 40".

From the binding fabric:

Cut 7 strips, 3" × 40".

From the hanging sleeve fabric:

Cut 2 strips, 8½" × 40".

assembling the quilt

Note:

Rows 1 and 3 of the checkerboard (top and bottom) begin and end with the dark fabric in the double position. Row 2 (the middle row) has the opposite configuration: it begins and ends with the light fabric in the double position.

ROW 1 AND ROW 3 CHECKERBOARDS

1. Sew 1 strip of light-value checkerboard fabric between 2 strips of Fat Quarter 1 dark-value checkerboard fabric along the long edges. Press toward the dark fabric. Make 2. Label them Set A. Crosscut into 13 segments, each 2″ wide.

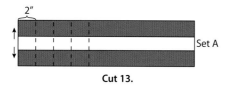

Cut 13.

2. Sew 1 strip of Fat Quarter 1 dark-value checkerboard fabric between 2 strips of light-value checkerboard fabric along the long edges. Press toward the dark fabric. Make 2. Label them Set B. Crosscut into 12 segments, each 2″ wide.

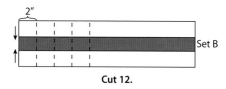

Cut 12.

3. Arrange the segments from Sets A and B as shown. Sew them together in 12 pairs as shown, then sew the pairs together.

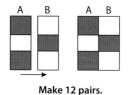

Make 12 pairs.

4. Sew a single segment from Set A to the end to make a row of 25 segments, 38″ long. Press all the seams in the same direction.

5. Repeat Steps 1–4 with strips from Fat Quarter 3.

ROW 2 CHECKERBOARD

6. Repeat Steps 1 and 2 for the light-value checkerboard fabric and Fat Quarter 2 dark-value checkerboard fabric, except cut 12 segments from Set A and 13 segments from Set B.

7. Arrange the segments from Sets A and B as shown, and sew them together as described in Step 3. Sew a single segment from Set B to the end to make a row of 25 segments, 38″ long. Press all the seams in the same direction.

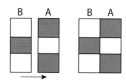

Make 12 pairs.

8. Place the 4 focus fabric sections on your design wall (see Design Play, page 78), or lay them out on a table or the floor. Place the 3 checkerboard units between them. Shift the focus fabrics from side to side until you find a position where the repeats are not directly above each other. When you're satisfied with the result, trim the focus fabrics to 38″, or the length of your checkerboard unit.

9. Stitch the focus fabric and checkerboard units together as shown in the assembly diagram. Press toward the focus fabric.

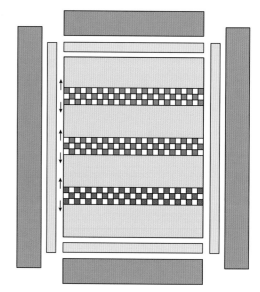

Assembly diagram

10. Referring to Adding Borders (page 79), sew the 2½″-wide inner borders to the top and bottom of the quilt top and then to the sides. Press the seams toward the border.

11. Repeat Step 10 to add the 6½″-wide outer borders.

finishing the quilt

Refer to pages 79–85 for more detailed information on finishing your quilt.

1. Prepare the backing.

2. Layer the quilt top, batting, and backing; baste.

3. Hand or machine quilt as desired.

4. Piece together the 3″-wide strips you cut from the binding fabric or left-over fat quarters to bind the edges of the quilt.

5. Add a hanging sleeve and label if desired.

Detail of *Prehistoric Playtime*

Prehistoric Playtime, 54″ × 62″,
made by Susie Kincy,
machine quilted by Barbara Dau, 2008.

Detail of *School Fun*

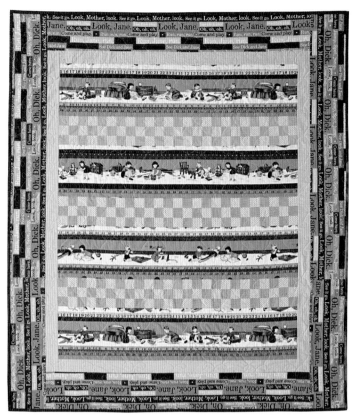

School Fun, 53″ × 60″, made by Vicki DeGraaf,
machine quilted by Doris Ellis, 2008.

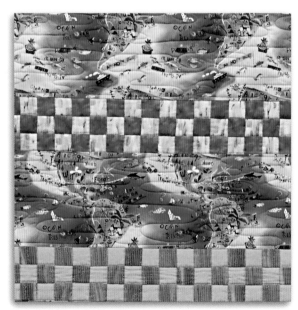

Detail of *Beautiful Blue Planet*

Beautiful Blue Planet, 53½″ × 61½″, made by Carla Zimmerman,
machine quilted by Arlene Anderson, 2008.

Detail of *School Daze*

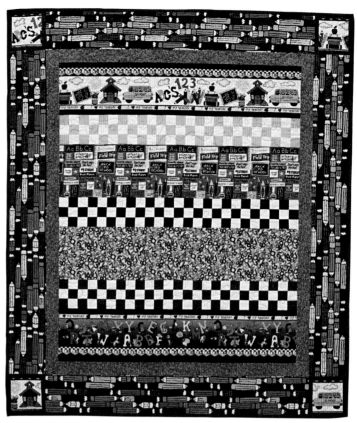

School Daze, 52½″ × 60″, made by John James,
machine quilted by Barbara Dau, 2008.

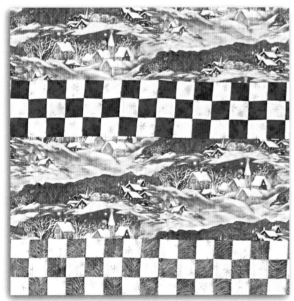

Detail of *Dashing Through the Snow*

Dashing Through the Snow, 56″ × 61″,
made and machine quilted by Cheryl Gilman, 2008.

play time *quilt*

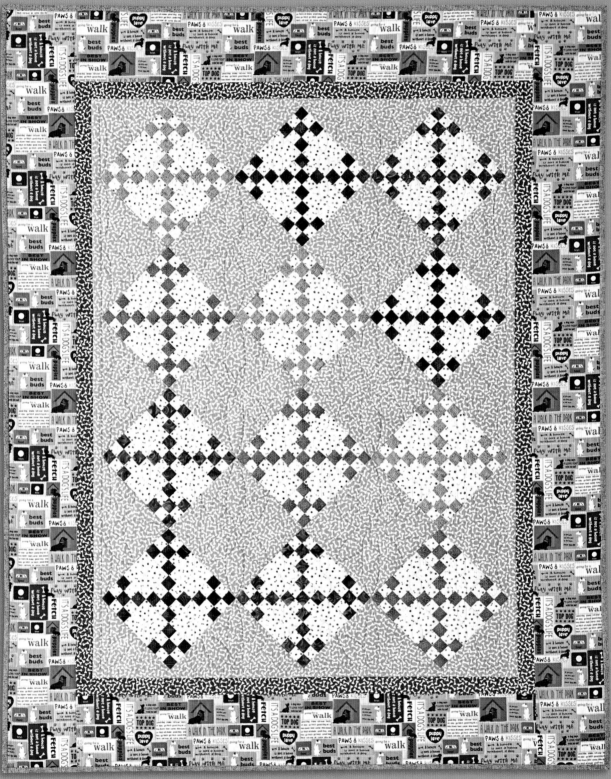

Best Friends!
Designed and made by M'Liss Rae Hawley,
machine quilted by Barbara Dau, 2008.

Finished quilt: 55¼″ × 68″
Finished block: 9″

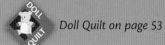

Doll Quilt on page 53

FAST, FAT QUARTER BABY QUILTS WITH M'LISS RAE HAWLEY

I've always loved this classic Double Nine-Patch pattern, although this is the first time I've included it in a book. I was so happy making the quilt that I made two—perfect for twins or for siblings close in age.

The traditional Double Nine-Patch gains child-style pizzazz when you add a playful border fabric. I selected favorite childhood themes. For *Best Friends!*, I used my *Good Dog* fabric collection. My *Giddy Up!* version (page 54) has a horse and cowboy theme. The colors as well as the themes in each are related. The borders share a color palette, and the colors in the Double Nine-Patch blocks repeat the border colors. Setting the blocks on point adds another element of liveliness.

With this project, I offer a special bonus—a matching doll quilt! This mini-quilt makes a cute companion gift for a new baby or a thoughtful gift for his or her sibling. It's also a creative way to use your leftover strip sets and fabric from the full-size quilt. For guidance, see Make a Matching Doll Quilt! (page 53).

materials

Fat quarters require 17½" × 20" of usable fabric. All other yardages are based on 40"-wide fabric.

▨ Fat quarters of 4 assorted fabrics

▨ 1¼ yards of fabric for block backgrounds

▨ 2⅛ yards of fabric for setting squares and triangles

▨ ⅓ yard of fabric for inner border

▨ 1⅓ yards of fabric for outer border*

▨ ⅔ yard of fabric for binding

▨ 4⅜ yards of fabric for backing

▨ ½ yard of fabric for a hanging sleeve (optional)

▨ 63" × 76" piece of batting

Allow extra yardage for directional fabric.

 To make the matching doll quilt, buy an extra fat quarter, or use a coordinating fabric from your stash for the backing.

 To make the matching doll quilt, buy a 17½" × 17½" piece of diaper flannel for batting.

cutting

Cut along the 20" length of the fat quarters. For the remaining fabrics, cut strips on the crosswise grain (from selvage to selvage).

From each fat quarter:

Cut 8 strips, 1½" × 20".

From the background fabric for the blocks:

Cut 14 strips, 1½" × 40"; crosscut into 28 strips, 1½" × 20".

Cut 5 strips, 3½" × 40"; crosscut into 48 squares, 3½" × 3½".

From the setting-squares and setting-triangles fabric:

Cut 2 strips, 9½" × 40"; crosscut into 6 squares, 9½" × 9½".

Cut 2 strips, 16½" × 40"; crosscut into 3 squares, 16½" × 16½". Cut each square in half *twice* diagonally to make 4 quarter-square side-setting triangles (12 total). You will have 2 triangles left over.

Cut 2 squares, 12" × 12"; cut each square in half *once* diagonally to make 2 half-square corner triangles (4 total).

From the inner border fabric:

Cut 5 strips, 2" × 40".

From the outer border fabric:

Cut 6 strips, 6½" × 40".

From the binding fabric:

Cut 7 strips, 3" × 40".

From the hanging sleeve fabric:

Cut 2 strips, 8½" × 40".

making the blocks

This finished quilt includes 12 pieced blocks: 3 per fat quarter. Each pieced block is made up of 5 Nine-Patch blocks and 4 background squares.

 If you plan to make a matching doll quilt, make an additional block.

> **STAY ORGANIZED**
>
> Stack together strips and units of matching fat-quarter fabrics as you cut them. Label them 1, 2, 3, and 4.

1. Sew 1 of the 1½" × 20" background strips between 2 of the 1½" × 20" strips from Fat Quarter 1 along the long edges. Make 2 more strip sets to match. Press toward the dark fabric. Repeat with Fat Quarters 2, 3, and 4, for a grand total of 12 strip sets. Label them all Set A.

Make 3 for each fat quarter.

2. Crosscut 30 segments, each 1½" wide, from the Fat Quarter 1 Set A strips. Repeat with the Fat Quarter 2, 3, and 4 Set A strips, for a grand total of 120 segments.

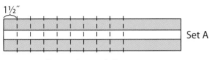

Cut 30 for each fat quarter.

3. Sew 1 of the 1½" × 20" strips from Fat Quarter 1 between 2 of the 1½" × 20" background strips, right sides together, along the long edges. Press toward the dark fabric. Make 1 more strip set to match. Repeat with strips from Fat Quarters 2, 3, and 4, for a grand total of 8 strip sets. Label them all Set B.

Make 2 for each fat quarter.

4. Crosscut 15 segments, each 1½" wide, from the Fat Quarter 1 Set B strips. Repeat with the Fat Quarter 2, 3, and 4 strip sets, for a grand total of 60 segments.

Cut 15 for each fat quarter.

5. Arrange the segments as shown; sew them together to make 15 Nine-Patch blocks of each fat quarter (a grand total of 60 blocks). Press away from the center, as shown. Each block should measure 3½" × 3½".

Set A Set B Set A
Make 15 for each fat quarter.

6. To make each pieced quilt block, arrange and sew together 5 matching Nine-Patch blocks and 4 background squares, 3½" × 3½", as shown, pressing the rows in opposite directions. Each block should measure 9½".

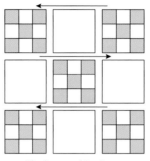

Block assembly diagram

assembling the quilt

The side and corner triangles are cut oversized so that the blocks appear to float. You will square up the quilt top after it is assembled.

1. Arrange the pieced blocks, setting squares, and side-setting triangles in a pleasing mix of fat-quarter blocks, in diagonal rows (on point), as shown in Assembly Diagram 1 (right). You will have 2 side-setting triangles left over.

2. Sew the blocks and setting squares together into diagonal rows. Press the pieced blocks toward the setting squares. Add the side-setting triangles. Press the seams toward the triangles. (You'll sew the corner-setting triangles in the next step.)

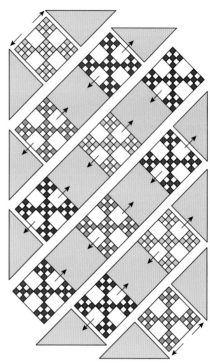

Assembly Diagram 1

3. Sew the rows together, carefully matching the seams. Press. Trim the dog ears at each corner, as shown in Assembly Diagram 2 (below). Sew the corner-setting triangles to the quilt top. Press the seams toward the triangles.

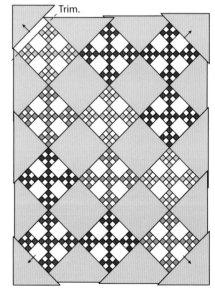

Assembly Diagram 2

4. Square up the quilt top, measuring 1" from the points of the blocks to trim the side and corner triangles.

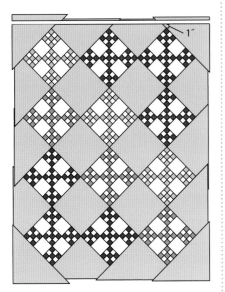

Trim triangles 1″ from block points.

5. Refer to Adding Borders (page 79) to measure, fit, and sew 2"-wide inner border strips to the top and bottom of the quilt. Press the seams toward the borders. Repeat to sew inner borders to the sides of the quilt.

6. Repeat Step 5 to add the 6½"-wide outer borders.

finishing the quilt

Refer to pages 79–85 for more detailed information on finishing your quilt.

1. Prepare the backing.

2. Layer the quilt top, batting, and backing; baste.

3. Hand or machine quilt as desired.

4. Piece together the 3"-wide strips you cut from the binding fabric to bind the edges of the quilt.

5. Add a hanging sleeve and label if desired.

MAKE A MATCHING DOLL QUILT!

Use the leftover strip sets you've already made, along with extra fabric from the quilt and from your fabric stash, to create a small-size replica of *Play Time*. Be sure to audition your fabrics to see how they work together.

The mini-quilt version features 1 Double Nine-Patch block in a straight set rather than on point. Referring to Steps 1–6 for the full-size quilt (page 51–52), make the following:

■ 1 Double Nine-Patch block, 9½″ × 9½″. (Use 1 Strip Set A and 1 Strip Set B, both from the same fat-quarter fabric, plus leftover background fabric.)

■ Use leftover setting-triangle fabric or other leftover fabric to make the inner border.

■ For the outer border and binding, use fabrics left over from the quilt, or new fabrics (purchased or from your stash).

■ Use an extra fat quarter or a coordinating fabric from your stash to make the backing.

■ From the inner border fabric, cut 2 strips, 1″ × 20″.

■ From the outer border fabric, cut 3 strips, 3″ × 20″.

■ From the binding fabric, cut 2 strips, $2^{7}/_{8}$″ × 40″.

■ Construct the borders, backing, and binding as described for the full-size quilt. The finished quilt will measure 15½″ × 15½″.

Best Friends Doll Quilt, 15½″ × 15½″, designed, made, and machine quilted by M'Liss Rae Hawley, 2008.

Giddy Up! Doll Quilt, 15½″ × 15½″,
designed, made, and machine quilted by M'Liss Rae Hawley, 2008.

Groovy Garden Doll Quilt, 15½″ × 15½″,
made and machine quilted by Susie Kincy, 2008.

Giddy Up! 55¼″ × 68″,
designed and made by M'Liss Rae Hawley,
machine quilted by Barbara Dau, 2008.

Groovy Garden, 55″ × 68″, made by Susie Kincy,
machine quilted by Barbara Dau, 2008.

Dragonflies in the Bamboo Doll Quilt, 15½˝ × 15½˝,
made and machine quilted by Cheryl Gilman, 2008.

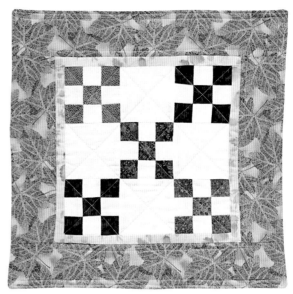

Purple-Lovers' Doll Quilt, 15˝ × 15˝,
made and machine quilted by Annette Barca, 2008.

Dragonflies in the Bamboo, 52˝ × 65½˝,
made by Cheryl Gilman,
machine quilted by Barbara Dau, 2008.

Love That Purple, 52˝ × 68˝,
made by Annette Barca,
machine quilted by Barbara Dau, 2008.

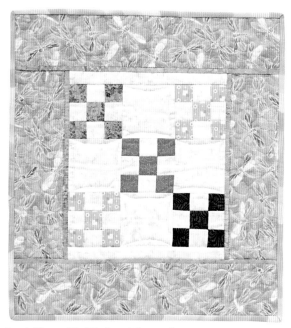

Buzzin' Around Doll Quilt, 15⅜″ × 16¾″,
made and machine quilted by Clara Hagglund, 2008.

Puddle Ducks Doll Quilt, 15″ × 15″,
made and machine quilted by John James, 2008.

Buzzin' Around, 54⅜″ × 66¾″,
made and machine quilted by Clara Hagglund, 2008.

Rainy Day Sunshine, 53½″ × 65½″,
made by John James,
machine quilted by Barbara Dau, 2008.

baby steps
doll quilt

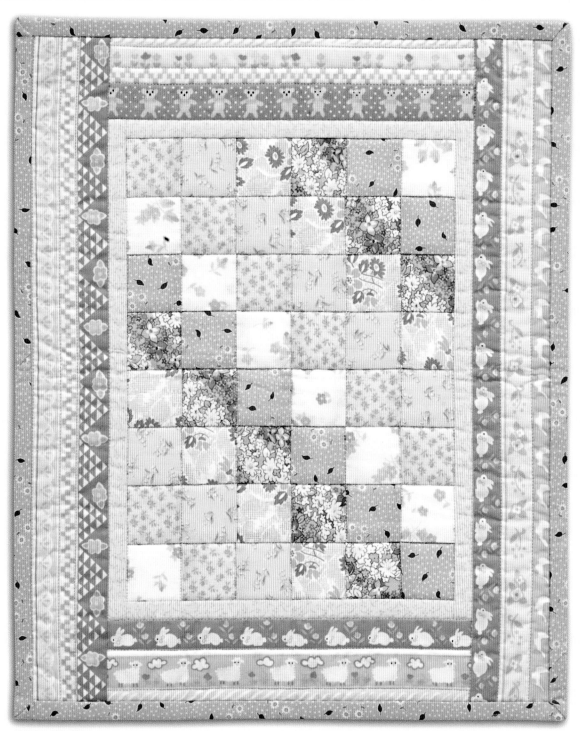

Nursery Medley
**Designed, made, and machine quilted
by M'Liss Rae Hawley, 2008.**

Finished quilt: 15½″ × 18½″
Finished block: 1½″

This is an easy little quilt that goes together quickly. It's such a charming gift idea for baby (and Mom) as a companion to one of the baby quilts in this book, for the new baby's sibling, or for any child (or grown-up doll collector)!

You can make this quilt from all-new fabrics you choose especially for this project. Or you can use your leftover fat-quarter, background, and border fabrics from the baby quilts to make a coordinating doll quilt. If you use these fabrics, be sure to audition them to see which ones go together to make a pleasing design. Small-scale prints work best. You'll undoubtedly want to visit your fabric stash to find additional ones that will complement and complete your quilt top; you probably have lots of other wonderful fabrics for a doll quilt. Check out all the great fabric themes in this book, and I'm sure you'll think of many more!

materials

Fat quarters require 17½" × 20" of usable fabric.

▦ 6 strips, 2" × 20", of assorted fat-quarter prints or 6 leftover print fabrics

▦ 3 strips, 1" × 20", of print fabric for the inner border

▦ 1 fat quarter for outer border

▦ 1 fat quarter for backing

▦ ¼ yard of fabric for binding

▦ 17½" × 20" piece of diaper flannel for batting

cutting

Cut along the 20" length of the fat quarters.

From each of 6 fat quarters:

Cut 1 strip, 2" × 20".

From the inner border fabric:

Cut 3 strips, 1" × 20".

From the outer border fabric:

Cut 3 strips, 3" × 20".

From the binding fabric:

Cut 3 strips, 2⅞" × 20".

assembling the quilt

1. Label your fat-quarter strips 1 through 6 and arrange them in a pleasing visual order on your design wall or on a table. Pin and sew the strips together.

| 6 |
| 5 |
| 4 |
| 3 |
| 2 |
| 1 |

Sew strips together.

2. Crosscut the strip set into 8 segments, each 2" wide.

Cut 8.

3. Arrange the segments in 8 columns as shown, starting at the left and moving right. In Column 1, Fabric 1 is at the bottom. For Column 2, use a seam ripper to remove Fabric 6 from the top, then sew that square to the Fabric 1 square so Fabric 6 is on the bottom. For Column 3, remove Fabrics 5 and 6 from the top, then sew them to the bottom. Continue through the 8 rows in this manner to create the stair-step effect. Press the rows in opposite directions.

1	2	3	4	5	6	7	8
6	5	4	3	2	1	6	5
5	4	3	2	1	6	5	4
4	3	2	1	6	5	4	3
3	2	1	6	5	4	3	2
2	1	6	5	4	3	2	1
1	6	5	4	3	2	1	6

4. Sew the rows together in order, carefully pinning the intersections to ensure an accurate match. Press. Rotate the finished quilt top to the position shown in the assembly diagram.

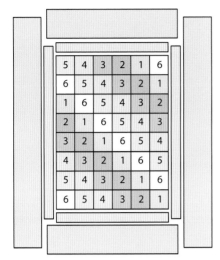

5	4	3	2	1	6
6	5	4	3	2	1
1	6	5	4	3	2
2	1	6	5	4	3
3	2	1	6	5	4
4	3	2	1	6	5
5	4	3	2	1	6
6	5	4	3	2	1

Assembly diagram

5. Refer to Adding Borders (page 79). Measure, trim, and sew the 1″-wide inner borders to the top and bottom of the quilt. Press the seams toward the borders. Repeat to sew borders to the sides.

6. Repeat Step 5 to add the 3″-wide outer borders.

finishing the quilt

Refer to pages 79–85 for more detailed information on finishing your quilt.

1. Prepare the backing.

2. Layer the quilt top, batting, and backing; baste.

3. Hand or machine quilt as desired.

4. Piece together the 2⅞″-wide strips you cut from 1 fat quarter to bind the edges of the quilt.

5. Add a label if desired.

Detail of Elegant Baby

Elegant Baby, 15½″ × 18½″,
designed, made, and machine quilted by M'Liss Rae Hawley, 2008

Dolly's Naptime, 17¼″ × 18¼″,
made and machine quilted by Carla Zimmerman, 2008.

Yellow and Blue á la 1930s, 15″ × 18½″,
made and machine quilted by Annette Barca, 2008.

Jason's Baby Steps, 17″ × 24″,
made and machine quilted by Susie Kincy, 2008.

Polka Dots, 19″ × 17½″,
made and machine quilted by Carla Zimmerman, 2008.

Michael's Baby Steps, 17″ × 24″,
made and machine quilted by Susie Kincy, 2008.

Rose Garden, 15½″ × 18½″,
made and machine quilted by Lucia Pan, 2008.

welcome home
layette set

So Sweet Layette Set, designed, made, and machine quilted by M'Liss Rae Hawley, 2008.

I think one of the best gifts you can make for a friend's or relative's new baby is something truly useful yet also pretty to look at. That's why I designed this three-piece set that features a receiving blanket, a shoulder cloth, and two bibs, all made in coordinating fabrics. You can make all the pieces in the set, or just one or two. In either case, tie them with a matching ribbon and present them in a cute basket or, if you're feeling ambitious, in one of the totes you can make from my book *101 Fabulous Fat Quarter Bags with M'Liss Rae Hawley*, available from C&T Publishing (see Resources, page 86).

receiving blanket

Finished size: 34" × 34"

Receiving Blanket, **designed, made, and machine quilted by M'Liss Rae Hawley, 2008.**

You can make this supersoft, cuddly blanket in a couple of hours to give as a shower gift or a last-minute coming-home present for a newborn.

Flannel is the fabric of choice for this project: it just gets softer the more it's used and washed. If your local quilt shop offers fat quarters of flannel, grab them (especially if they have baby- and child-friendly motifs and colors)! If you can't find flannel fat quarters or two to four flannels that coordinate well together, you can opt for cotton fat quarters in fun fabrics. Either way, back the blanket with flannel for that special soft touch. This simple pattern doesn't require batting; you just sew together the top and the backing, and—voilà—a blanket!

MATERIALS

Fat quarters require 17½" × 20" of usable fabric. All other yardages are based on 40"-wide fabric.

▦ 4 fat quarters or 2 half yards of assorted flannels* or cottons

▦ 1⅛ yards of flannel for backing

Be sure to prewash flannel—it may shrink and ravel!

CUTTING

From fat quarters or half yards:

Cut 4 squares, 17½" × 17½".

From the backing:

Cut 1 square, 34½" × 34½".

MAKING THE BLANKET

1. To make the blanket top, place the four 17½" × 17½" squares in a pleasing arrangement. Sew them together. Press.

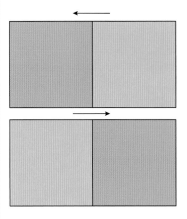

2. Pin the blanket top and backing right sides together, with all the edges matching. Leave a 6-inch opening at one end. Stitch all around, using a ¼" seam allowance. Press. Clip the corners.

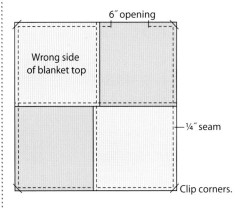

3. Turn the blanket right side out, and hand stitch the opening closed. Press.

4. Topstitch ¼" all around the edges (see Plan Ahead, below) using a straight stitch or a decorative stitch of your choice.

Topstitch using decorative stitch for embellishment.

5. Refer to Selecting and Marking Quilting Designs (page 79) to machine quilt in the ditch along the vertical and horizontal seams.

PLAN AHEAD

Be sure to fill your sewing machine bobbin before you begin decorative stitching around the outside edge of the blanket. I used the same color thread in the bobbin and in the needle. If you're using flannel, test your decorative stitch on a scrap piece first to make sure it looks the way you want it to.

shoulder cloth

Finished size: 17" × 12"

Shoulder Cloth, **designed and made by M'Liss Rae Hawley, 2008.**

This project couldn't be simpler: just stitch together two layers of soft flannel, and you're done. You can use the same fabrics you used for the receiving blanket, or choose different coordinating fabrics. Or make one to match a baby quilt you've made.

Make as many of these practical shoulder cloths as you wish. No parent can have too many.

MATERIALS

Fat quarters require 17½" × 20" of usable fabric.

■ 1 fat quarter of flannel for front

■ 1 fat quarter of flannel for back

CUTTING

From each fat quarter:

Cut 1 rectangle, 12½" × 17½".

MAKING THE SHOULDER CLOTH

1. Place the 2 fat quarters, right sides together, on your cutting mat. With a fabric-marking pencil or chalk, draw a curve on one side of the long edge. Along the other long side, draw another curve that's a parallel image. Using your rotary cutter, follow the lines to trim the fabric.

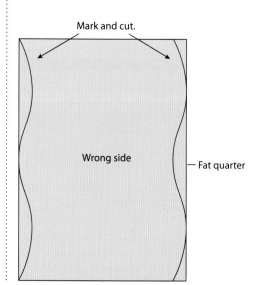

2. Pin the 2 layers right sides together with all edges matching. Stitch all around, using a ¼" seam allowance. Leave a 5" opening at one end. Press. Clip the corners.

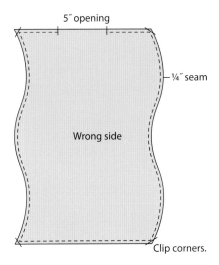

3. Turn the shoulder cloth right side out, and hand stitch the opening closed. Press.

4. Topstitch ¼" all around the edges, using a straight stitch or a decorative stitch of your choice.

Topstitch using decorative stitch for embellishment.

bib

Finished size: 7¾" × 9¾"

Makes 2 bibs.

Bibs, designed, made, and machine quilted by M'Liss Rae Hawley, 2008.

These simple bibs are made from two fat-quarter fabrics that coordinate with the fabrics you select for the receiving blanket and shoulder cloth. Use flannel, regular cotton, or both for two great reversible bibs. To use the pattern provided on page 67, copy it on a copy machine at 100%, and cut it out.

MATERIALS

Fat quarters require 17½" × 20" of usable fabric.

▧ 1 fat quarter of flannel or cotton for 2 bibs

▧ 1 fat quarter of flannel or cotton for backing

▧ 1 fat quarter of lightweight, light-colored cotton for batting

▧ 1 package (4 yards) ¼" double-fold bias tape in a contrasting or coordinating color for binding

CUTTING

From each fat quarter:

Cut 1 rectangle, 12″ × 20″.*

*_Check the motif or pattern on the fabric; if it is directional, you may want to cut it the other way._

MAKING THE BIB

1. Layer the three 12″ × 20″ rectangles: place the backing right side down, place the batting over it, and add the top, right side up. Hand baste or pin the 3 layers together (or use a spray adhesive), to make reversible bib fabric. Machine quilt the layers together as described in Quilting Your Quilt (pages 81–82), using a meander stitch, a grid, or whichever pattern you wish.

Machine quilt the layers.

2. Pin the bib pattern (page 67) on the quilted fabric and cut out 2 bibs.

3. To bind the bibs, sew the bias tape along the outside edge of each bib as described in Refresher Course: Bias Binding (below). When you get to the end, cut off the tape even with the bib's neck edges.

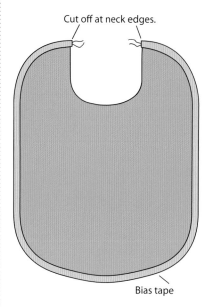

4. To make the tie, cut a 27″ piece of bias tape, and fold it in half to find the center. Match the center of the tape to the center of the neck edge. Pin. Begin stitching at one shoulder, covering the raw end of the tape you've already stitched to the bib's outside edge.

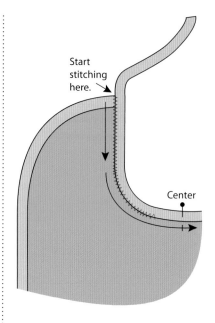

5. Stitch around the neck, and continue stitching together the edges of the tape to the end of the first tie as shown below. Now go back and stitch the other tie from the neck edge to the end. To finish the ends of the ties, fold them in ½″ and stitch across the ends, or tie each end in a knot.

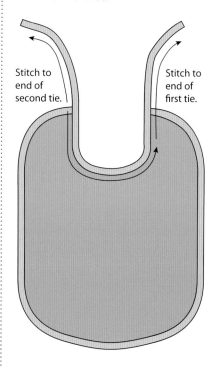

REFRESHER COURSE: BIAS BINDING

If you need to practice stitching a binding of bias tape, use a piece of leftover quilted fabric and a few inches of the bias tape.

■ Place the fabric right side up, and fold the bias tape over the raw edge with the narrower side of the tape on top. It may help to pin it in place.

■ Topstitch the tape in place along the edge, making sure to catch the tape on the underside too. I use a small zigzag or straight stitch with cotton thread in a matching color.

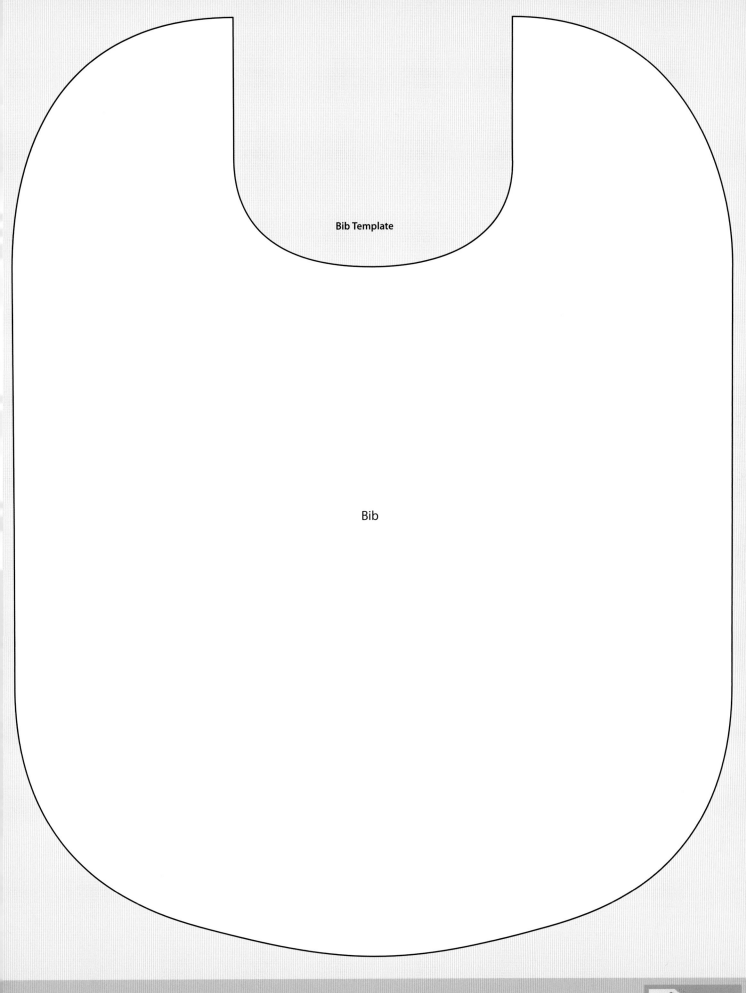

Bib Template

Bib

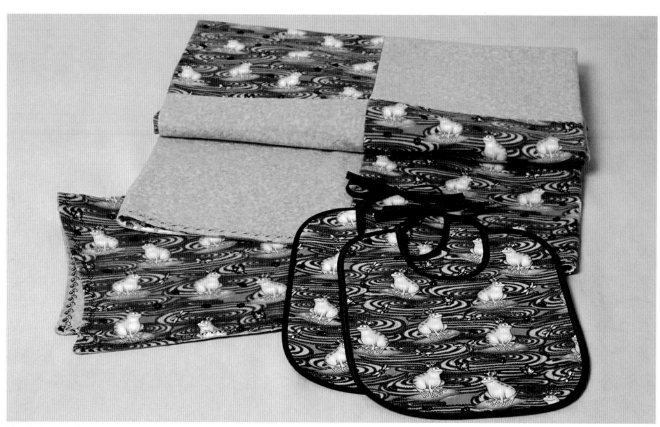

Kiss Me Layette Set,
designed, made, and machine quilted by M'Liss Rae Hawley, 2008.

Bunny Layette Set,
designed, made, and machine quilted by John and Louise James, 2008.

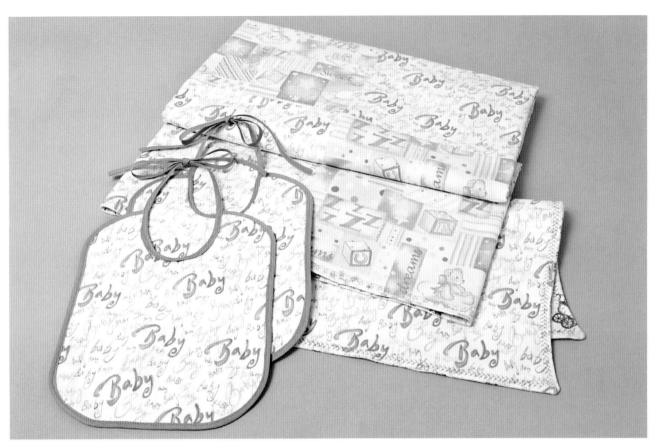

Baby Boy Blue Layette Set,
designed, made, and machine quilted by John and Louise James, 2008.

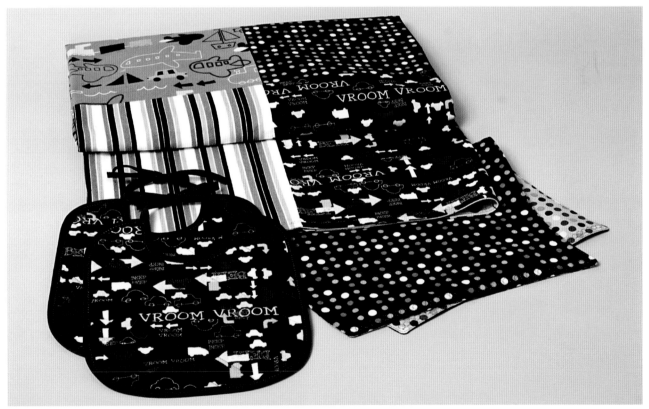

Beep Beep! Layette Set,
designed, made, and machine quilted by Susie Kincy, 2008.

panel quilt
in an afternoon

Kelsey Creek Farm
Designed, made, and machine quilted by
M'Liss Rae Hawley, 2008.

 Finished size: Approximately
36" × 41", depending on
panel size

FAST, FAT QUARTER BABY QUILTS WITH M'LISS RAE HAWLEY

Yes, you *can* make this quick-and-easy baby quilt in *one afternoon!*

It makes a charming wallhanging as well as a quilt. If you happen to find a preprinted panel you love, like the farm scene in my quilt, or an adorable baby fabric (especially one with a large-scale novelty print), you have a reason to buy it.

You'll want to make lots of these panel quilts! You can even make multiple quilts from the same fabric to give to children's charities. I love this project, and I've made hundreds for family, friends, and charities. I make them as a little break in between my book projects. When someone has a baby or requests a quilt for a local charity or for an orphanage overseas, I have quilts ready to go.

materials

Yardages are based on 40″-wide fabric.

■ 1 yard of fabric, or 1 preprinted panel (usually about a yard)

■ 1⅛ yards of coordinating flannel for backing

■ 2 strips, 2″ × 44″, of muslin or coordinating fabric for spacer strips

■ 42″ × 48″ piece of batting

■ 1 package of 2″-wide satin blanket binding

■ 1 or 2 strips of fabric, 8½″ × 40″, for a hanging sleeve (optional)

making the quilt

1. If you're using a preprinted panel, you'll want to make sure that when you add the binding, it won't cover up the edges of the panel's design. To do this, stitch a spacer (a 2″-wide strip of muslin or matching fabric) along the sides of the panel where the design ends so that you'll have an even amount of fabric around the outside edge. (Most panels are printed so they have a sufficient allowance along the top and bottom.)

Add a spacer strip to the sides.

2. Layer the quilt top, batting, and backing, referring to Preparing Your Quilt for Quilting, page 79. Machine quilt as described in Artful Quilting (page 72).

3. Square up the quilt, referring to Squaring Up and Trimming (page 82). Pay careful attention to measuring around the edges, so that you have a border the width of the binding on all sides where none of the panel design will be covered up.

4. Using a serpentine stitch, sew all around the quilt ¼″ from the edge to hold all 3 layers together. If your binding is a light color, use a thread color that won't show through.

5. Thread your sewing machine with thread that matches the blanket binding. Beginning at a midpoint on the bottom of the quilt, fold the binding over the raw edge, and pin.

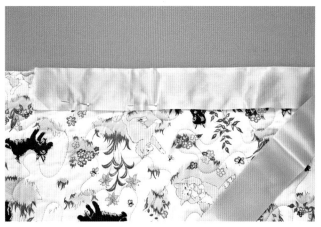

Pin blanket binding to quilt.

6. Begin sewing the binding, using a serpentine stitch. Make sure to catch the binding's edges on both the front and back of the quilt. As you approach the corner, take the quilt out of the machine. Miter the corner by folding diagonally as shown. Pin it carefully, and put the corner back under the needle.

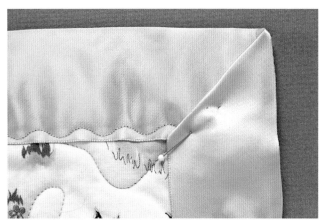

Miter binding corner by folding diagonally.

7. Begin sewing at the top edge of the point. Sew down to the inner corner, and continue sewing along the binding.

Sew binding from top edge of point to inner corner.

PROTECT THOSE CORNERS!

When you stitch the corners of your satin blanket binding, the feed dogs on your machine can snag it. Here's my trick: Before I put my needle down on each corner, I put a scrap of fabric underneath, and—no more snags!

8. Repeat Steps 6 and 7 for all 4 corners. When you come to the end, take the quilt out of the machine. Fold the end of the binding under, overlapping at least an inch, and machine stitch to finish.

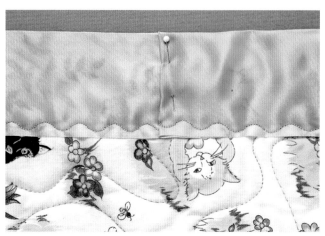

At the end, fold under and stitch closed.

9. Add a label to the back of your quilt as described in Creating a Label (page 85).

ARTFUL QUILTING

On a preprinted panel or a fabric with a large-scale motif, you can enhance the motifs by outline quilting, following the designs on the panel or fabric, as I did on *Magic Castle* (page 73). Or you can use an allover design, like a meandering stipple stitch, or make a simple grid (see Quilting Your Quilt, page 81). Use colorful cotton or rayon thread.

The outline quilting in *Magic Castle* (page 73) does wonders to enhance the panel's motifs.

Magic Castle, 36˝ × 42˝, designed, made, and machine quilted by M'Liss Rae Hawley, 2008.

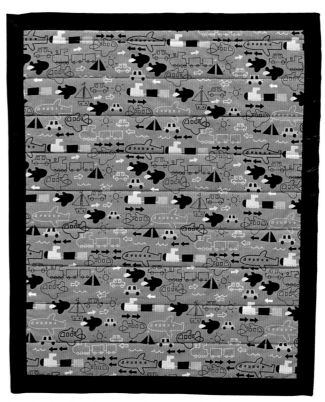

Beep Beep!, 34˝ × 41˝, made and machine quilted by Susie Kincy, 2008.

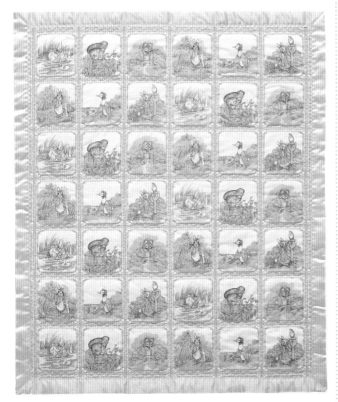

Vintage Beatrix Potter, 36˝ × 43˝, designed, made, and machine quilted by M'Liss Rae Hawley, 2008.

Butterflies and Flowers, 35½˝ × 40½˝, made and machine quilted by Susie Kincy, 2008.

putting it all together

This section includes the basics of cutting and assembling the pieces, units, and blocks in your quilt, as well as quilting and finishing the quilt.

The fat-quarter quilts and other projects in this book are generally easy to make. I've streamlined the instructions to take advantage of the various rotary-cutting and quick-piecing techniques we quiltmakers have come to know and rely on.

rotary cutting

The process for rotary cutting fat quarters is pretty much the same as for cutting yardage, except the fabric pieces are smaller. The following guidelines work for both.

Note:

Cutting instructions are for right-handers. Reverse if you are left-handed.

SQUARING UP YOUR FABRIC

Square the edges of your fabrics before rotary cutting them into strips and smaller pieces. Squaring is especially important with fat quarters. The pieces of fabric are small, and every inch is precious. The instructions for each project tell you which edge of the fat quarter to cut.

Press the fabric, and fold it carefully before you begin. You need to fold a fat quarter only once. Fold larger pieces twice, or break them down so that you can work with a more manageable amount.

1. Place the folded fabric on the cutting mat with the fold closest to you.

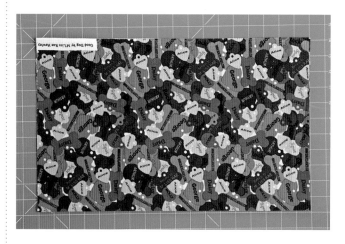

2. Position your ruler on the right-hand edge of the fabric so that the ruler is perpendicular to the fold. Trim a narrow strip from the right-hand edge of the fabric to square it up.

3. Rotate the fabric (or the mat) 180°, and repeat Step 2 at the opposite edge.

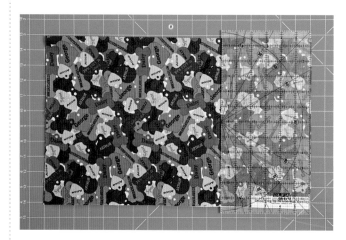

CUTTING STRIPS AND PIECES

Whether you are cutting fat quarters or yardage, use the lines on your ruler, not on your mat, to measure and cut the strips and pieces. Use the mat grid only for aligning the fabric and taking rough measurements.

1. Working from the squared left edge of the fabric, measure and cut a strip of the desired width. Repeat to cut the required number of strips. You may need to square up the end after every few cuts.

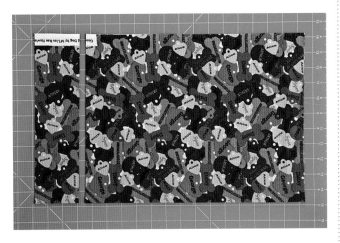

2. Cut the strips into squares or other smaller segments as directed in the project instructions.

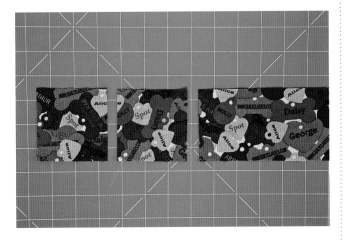

CUTTING TRIANGLES

Some quilt blocks, like those in *Motion Commotion* (page 38), contain half-square triangles. In a half-square triangle, the straight grain (lengthwise and crosswise) falls on the 2 short sides of the shape, and the long diagonal edge falls on the stretchy bias.

Begin by cutting squares as described in Cutting Strips and Pieces (left). Use your rotary cutter and ruler to divide each square from corner to corner in one direction. Each square yields 2 half-square triangles with the straight of grain (lengthwise and crosswise) on the 2 short sides.

piecing

Use a ¼" seam allowance for piecing the quilts in this book. (All cut measurements include a ¼" seam allowance.)

Sewing an accurate ¼" seam is *essential* if you want the pieces, units, blocks, and borders of your quilt top to fit together. It's always a good idea to check that your ¼" seam is accurate before beginning to sew.

TESTING YOUR SEAM ALLOWANCE

Cut 2 strips of scrap fabric, each 1½″ × 3½″. With right sides together, sew the strips together along one 3½″ side. Carefully press the seam in one direction, and measure the finished unit. It should measure exactly 2½″ wide. If it does not, try again until you are able to sew a perfect ¼″ seam.

CREATING A ¼″ GUIDE

Here's a quick solution that will adapt your machine for precise piecing if your presser foot does not measure an exact ¼″ seam. Place your acrylic rotary-cutting ruler under the needle, lower the presser foot, and drop the needle so it lands exactly on the ruler's ¼″ marking. Place a piece of masking tape (or blue painter's tape for a more temporary solution) on the throat plate of the machine, right along the edge of the ruler. This will be your guide for lining up the raw edges of your fabric pieces to sew a perfect seam!

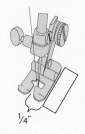

¼″

time-savers

You'll love these fast and easy techniques. They not only save time, but also help you improve your accuracy.

PIECING PERFECT POINTS THE EASY WAY

Sometimes when sewing units together, previously sewn seams can be your guide to perfect points. For example, when sewing the units in the *Motion Commotion* pinwheel block (page 38), you'll notice that the seams create an X. You can use this to your advantage when it is time to join one half of the pinwheel block to the other half. Sew the 2 pieces together just 1 thread beyond the X. You'll love the results!

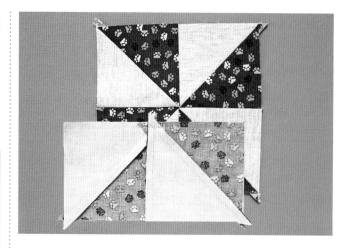

STARTER SCRAPS FOR EASY FABRIC FEEDING

Starter scraps are little pieces of fabric that, when used at the beginning of your piecing, will prevent your machine from gobbling the little triangle corners of your fabric. This technique works both on single pieces and in chain piecing. Begin your stitching on a small starter scrap before feeding onto the real thing. Works every time!

STRIP PIECING

This technique comes in handy when you need to sew squares and/or rectangles together to make multiple identical units, such as the checkerboard units in *Opportunity Quilt* (page 44), or the blocks for *First Steps* (page 32). Instead of sewing individual pieces together over and over, you sew strips together to make strip sets, or strata; "slice" or crosscut the sets into segments; and then rearrange and sew the segments together to complete the unit.

1. With right sides together, sew the strips together along their long edges in the order given in the project instructions. Press the seams as shown in the accompanying diagram.

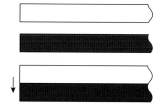

2. Use your rotary cutter and ruler to cut segments from the strip set in the width given in the project instructions.

3. Proceed to arrange and assemble the segments as described in the project instructions.

CHAIN PIECING

This technique saves time and thread when you need to stitch a series of identical pieces or units together. Simply feed and stitch the units one after another, without lifting the presser foot or cutting the thread in between. When you are finished, remove the "chain" from the machine and clip the threads in between to separate the units.

Chain piecing

making the blocks

Generally, to make blocks you'll sew pieces into units and units into rows. Then you'll sew the rows together to complete each block, as with *Baby's Windows* (page 16).

For each pattern in this book, I'll tell you which way to press the seams, either in the instructions themselves or with arrows in the accompanying diagrams.

Typically you will press toward the darker fabric or in the opposite direction from the adjacent units so the seams "nest" nicely when you match and pin them for sewing.

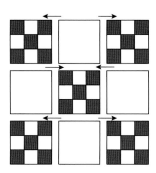

Note:

In most cases, piecing diagrams show finished units and blocks—that is, without the seam allowances.

For perfect block assembly, follow these tips:

▦ Place all pieces, units, and rows right sides together for assembly.

▦ Align raw edges as described in the project instructions.

▦ Use those pins! When joining units into rows and joining rows together, pin to match the seams and ends first, then add extra pins as needed.

▦ If one piece, unit, or row is slightly larger than the other, pin as usual and then sew with the larger piece on the bottom and against the throat plate of the machine. The action of the feed dogs will help ease the larger piece to fit.

▦ Press each seam as you sew it. Press lightly with a lifting-and-lowering motion. Dragging the iron across the fabric can distort the individual pieces and finished blocks.

squaring the blocks

It's important that all your blocks are the same size in order for the pieces of the quilt top to fit together and for your finished quilt to be flat and square. Here's how to make your blocks uniform:

Measure each block. The unfinished measurement—that is, the measurement before the block is sewn into the quilt top—should be the size indicated at the beginning of the instructions for each pattern plus ½".

If your blocks vary by less than ¼", use your rotary cutter and ruler to trim the larger blocks to match the smaller ones. Take care not to cut off any outside points (such as tips of triangles) and to maintain a ¼" seam allowance all around the outer edge of the block. To keep the block square, divide the excess measurement and remove an equal amount from all four sides, as shown.

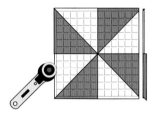

If any block varies by more than ¼" in size from the others, I suggest you remake that block. Before you begin, refer to Testing Your Seam Allowance (page 76) to retest your ¼" seam for accuracy.

assembling the quilt top

Different quilt patterns call for different *settings*. A setting refers to how the units or blocks are arranged and put together.

In a *straight set*, the blocks are arranged in horizontal rows, with the block edges parallel to the sides of the quilt. The blocks are sewn together with ¼" seam allowances to create the rows, and the seams are pressed in opposite directions from row to row. Then the rows are sewn together, and the seams are pressed, usually in one direction. *Building Blocks* (page 23) and *Motion Commotion* (page 38) are examples of straight sets.

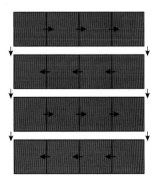

In a *diagonal or on-point set*, the blocks are arranged in diagonal rows, with the block edges at a 45° angle to the sides of the quilt. The zigzag edges are filled in with half- and quarter-square triangles to straighten the edges of the quilt top. (The project instructions tell you how many of these triangles to cut and how big to cut them.) The blocks and side triangles are sewn together with ¼" seam allowances to create the diagonal rows, with the seams pressed in opposite directions from row to row. The corner triangles are added next, and finally the rows are sewn together and pressed. *Play Time* (page 50) is a perfect example.

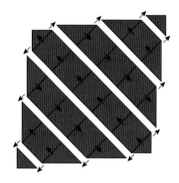

A *coins set* quilt is assembled in rows instead of blocks. Then the rows are sewn together, often with strips of sashing between the rows and with the seams pressed toward the sashing strips. *Opportunity Quilt* (page 44) is assembled as a coins set.

DESIGN PLAY

Before deciding on the final layout of your quilt top, rearrange the blocks several times to create a pleasing visual balance and to make sure you have the design that you like best. Many quilters create a design wall on which to "play" with various arrangements. Although you can lay out your blocks for a small quilt on a large tabletop or on the floor, I love my design wall—I use it every day!

I made my design wall by sandwiching heavyweight cotton batting between two double-size white flannel sheets. I machine quilted it with a 4" grid, and I serged around the edges. My husband, Michael, attached a store-bought wooden quilt hanger to my studio wall and placed the design wall in the holder.

adding borders

All of the quilts in this book feature squared borders. The good news is that these are the easiest of all borders to sew!

1. Measure the finished quilt top through the center from side to side. Sew border strips together as necessary. Cut 2 borders to this measurement for top and bottom borders.

2. Place pins at the center of the top and bottom of the quilt top, as well as at the midpoint of each border strip. Pin the borders to the quilt top, matching the ends and center points. Use additional pins as needed, easing or gently stretching the border to fit. Sew the borders to the quilt top with a ¼″ seam allowance. Press as instructed—usually toward the borders.

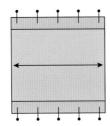

3. Measure the quilt from top to bottom, including the borders you've just sewn. Cut 2 borders to this measurement for the side borders. Repeat Step 2 to pin, sew, and press the borders.

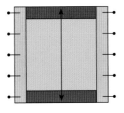

preparing your quilt for quilting

Don't skimp in preparing your quilt for quilting! Take the time to layer it properly and baste it sufficiently so that it will be free of puckers and bumps.

Carefully press the quilt top from the back to set the seams, and then press from the front. If you wish, use spray starch or sizing. Use a pair of small scissors or snips to trim any stray threads that may shadow through to the front of the quilt.

SELECTING AND MARKING QUILTING DESIGNS

A quilt becomes a quilt when it includes three layers—a top, a layer of batting, and a backing—all secured with stitching of some type to hold the layers together. (This means that to call your project a quilt, you need to finish it!) Besides, quilting stitches add a new and exciting dimension of design and texture to your quilt.

Some quilters stitch by hand; others, by machine. My quilts in this book—as well as almost all the quilts made by my wonderful group of quilters—were machine quilted.

Each step of the quiltmaking process, including the machine quilting, is exciting and fun to me. I love the idea of adding yet another level of creativity to my quilts. Machine quilting my own tops gives me flexibility in making those design decisions, and I do my own quilting whenever I can. Because of time constraints, however, I find I must now have many of my quilt tops professionally machine quilted.

Sources for quilting designs are everywhere. Explore the many choices available in quilting magazines and quilting pattern books, as well as quilting stencils. Examine your fabrics; perhaps there is a motif or pattern you can outline or adapt for quilting.

Depending on the kind of quilting design you're using, you may or may not need to mark the quilt top before you baste the layers together.

Options that *don't* require marking are:

■ quilting in the ditch (right beside the seamlines), whether by hand or machine;

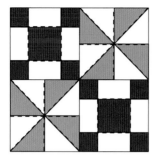

■ outline quilting (stitching ¼" inside each shape), whether by hand or machine; and

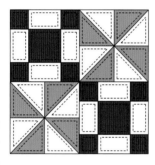

■ stipple quilting by machine (some forms), as described in Quilting Your Quilt (page 81).

Most other quilting designs are best marked on your quilt top before you baste the layers together. Use a tool made for marking fabric, such as chalk, a water-soluble marker, or a silver pencil. Always test any marking tool on scraps of your fabrics to be sure you can remove the marks easily after you've finished quilting.

Preparing the Batting and Backing

The choice of batting is a personal decision, but you'll want to consider the method (and amount) of quilting you plan to do, as well as the quilt's end use. I recommend machine quilting for babies' and children's quilts, for the simple reason that it's strong enough to stand up to all that loving wear and tear over the years. For machine quilting, I usually use cotton batting in a heavier weight (any product identified as "extra" or "ultra" loft, such as Quilters Dream batting, deluxe weight) for

bed quilts and wallhangings. (If you do hand quilt, stick with lightweight or low-loft batting.) No matter which type of batting you use, cut it approximately 4" larger than the quilt top on all sides.

Cut your backing the same size as the batting. If you need to piece the backing, the cut yardage specified for the projects in this book is enough to enable you to make vertical seams. Prewash the backing fabric and remove the selvages first.

SPECIAL BATTING CHOICES

For light-colored quilts, always choose white batting that won't show through.

For very small quilts, like the doll quilts in this book, use soft, pliable diaper flannel instead of quilt batting.

Layering and Basting

Unlike many machine quilters, I prefer to hand baste with thread rather than pin baste.

1. Carefully press the quilt top as described above. Press the backing. If you wish, use spray starch or sizing.

2. Spread the backing wrong side up on a clean, flat surface, and secure it with masking tape. The fabric should be taut but not stretched. Center the batting over the backing. Finally, center the quilt top right side up over the batting.

3. Thread a long needle with light-colored thread. Beginning in the center of the quilt, stitch a 4" grid of horizontal and vertical lines.

4. Remove the tape, and get ready to quilt.

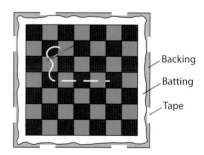

Backing

Batting

Tape

quilting your quilt

Quilting is an art form, so there is a learning curve involved. Practice is the best way to learn and master this skill. For details on hand quilting, consult one of the many books available at your local quilt store. If, like me, you want to machine quilt, you'll need a special attachment or two for your sewing machine, plus some tips. Here are some guidelines to get you started.

DUAL-FEED FOOT

The dual-feed foot is designed to hold and feed the three layers of your quilt evenly as you stitch. Use this foot to machine quilt single lines or parallel lines and grids—whether vertical, horizontal, or diagonal.

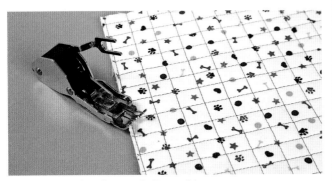

Use a dual-feed foot for straight-line quilting.

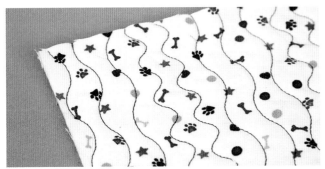

You can also use the dual-feed foot to make a simple serpentine stitch.

OPEN-TOE STIPPLING FOOT

Also called a darning foot, the open-toe stippling foot allows you to quilt in all directions: you are the guide! Use this foot for following fabric motifs, quilting curved designs, meander quilting (just what it sounds like!), and other free-motion techniques. I like to stipple quilt around machine-embroidered motifs, because the many meandering lines of heavy quilting cause the embroidered design to pop out and become a focal point.

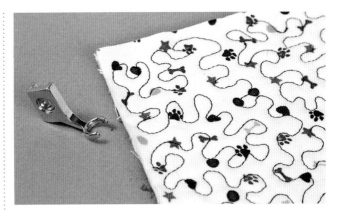

Use an open-toe foot for free-motion quilting.

You will need to drop the feed dogs on your sewing machine when you use the open-toe stippling foot. You might also need to set the presser foot pressure to the darning position so you can move the quilt at a smooth pace for consistent stitches. Some machines have a built-in stipple stitch, which is a wonderful way to achieve this beautiful surface texture.

THREADS

I consider quilting thread to be a design element, not just the means to hold the three layers of my quilts together. I also believe that variety in thread adds visual interest and showcases the quilter's individuality. For these reasons, I frequently use a mix of threads in my quilts. When choosing thread, I consider thread color, texture, and weight as well as where I plan to use the thread.

Typical thread choices for machine quilting include rayon (35- and 40-weight), cotton, and polyester. I use lots of variegated and metallic threads, as well as novelty threads.

If you want to do your quilting by hand, use 100% cotton thread in the color of your choice.

I use a wide variety of threads in my quilts.

DESIGN

To begin, anchor key seams in and around blocks and borders by stitching in the ditch along the seamlines. It's also a great idea, if you're a beginner, to stitch a simple grid of vertical and horizontal or diagonal lines to cover the quilt top's entire surface.

If you're comfortable with using the open-toe machine foot, try filling in open spaces with loops, curves, clamshells, and waves. Combine straight and curvy lines for variety.

One simple design option is to let your stitching follow the fabric motif—especially effective in a large-scale background fabric or outer border fabric. I also like to pull a motif such as stars or wagon wheels from fabric in one area of the quilt and adapt it for quilting in another area.

In *Giddy Up!* (page 54), I used a lariat quilting motif—perfect for the cowboy theme.

Another option is to explore the many choices available in quilting stencils and books of quilting patterns. With these, you can create quilted designs like those in Peggy Johnson's *Butterflies, Dragonflies & Bumblebees, Oh My!* (page 30).

I love to use heavy free-motion quilting, such as stippling, in the backgrounds behind pieced and embroidered motifs. Heavy quilting causes the background to recede and the motif to pop forward, taking center stage in the design.

Note how the heavily quilted background in the blocks of *Spring View Embroidery* (page 9) makes the embroideries seem to pop.

applying the finishing touches

The binding, hanging sleeve, and label of your quilt are important too, so be sure to give them the same attention you've given to every other element.

SQUARING UP AND TRIMMING

Before adding the binding, you need to trim the excess batting and backing and square up your quilt. Use the seams of the outer borders as a guide.

1. Align a ruler with the outer-border seam, and measure to the edge of the quilt in several places. Use the narrowest measurement as a guide for positioning your ruler, and use a rotary cutter to trim the excess batting and backing all around the quilt.

2. Fold the quilt in half lengthwise and crosswise to check that the corners are square and that the sides are equal in length. If they aren't, use a large square ruler to even them up, one corner at a time.

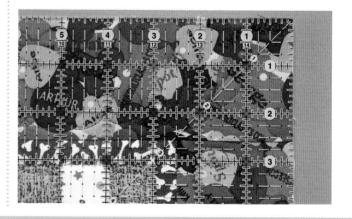

3. Stabilize the quilt edges by stitching around the perimeter with a basting or serpentine stitch. (Do not use a zigzag stitch—it can push and pull the fabric out of shape.) A dual-feed foot works well for this.

4. Remove any stray threads or bits of batting from the quilt top. You are now ready to bind your quilt.

MAKING AND APPLYING BINDING

Binding is an important and, sadly, often overlooked step in the quiltmaking process. Many a wonderful quilt is spoiled by a poorly sewn binding. Take your time deciding what fabric you will use, and enjoy the process of stitching it to your quilt. You're coming down the home stretch now!

Typically, I cut binding strips 3″ wide from selvage to selvage across the width of the fabric. I make an exception and cut strips on the bias only when I want to create a special effect with a plaid or striped fabric, or when I need to follow a curved or rounded edge.

The following method is the one I use to bind my quilts. It results in a finished edge that is attractive and strong.

1. Cut enough binding strips to go around the perimeter (outside edges) of the quilt, plus an extra 10″–12″ for seams and corners. Sew the strips together at right angles, as shown. Trim the excess fabric from the seams, leaving a ¼″ seam allowance, and press the seams open.

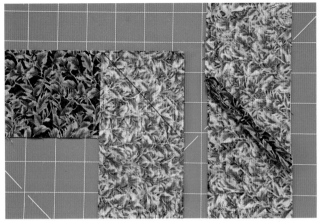

2. Fold the binding in half lengthwise, wrong sides together, and press.

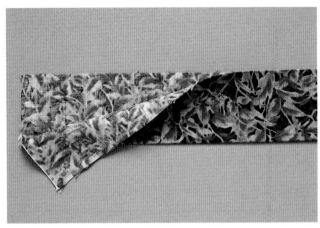

3. Starting 8″ down from the upper right corner and with the raw edges even, place the binding on the quilt top. Check to see that none of the diagonal seams falls on a corner of the quilt. If one does, adjust the starting point. Begin stitching 4″ from the end of the binding, using a ½″ seam allowance.

4. Stitch about 2″ and then stop and cut the threads. Remove the quilt from the machine and fold the binding to the back of the quilt. The binding should cover the line of machine stitching on the back. If the binding overlaps the stitching too much, try again, taking a slightly wider seam allowance. If the binding doesn't cover the original line of stitching, take a slightly narrower seam allowance. Remove the unwanted stitches before you continue.

5. Using the stitching position you determined in Step 4, resume stitching until you are ½" from the first corner of the quilt. Stop, backstitch, cut the thread, and remove the quilt from the machine.

6. Fold the binding straight up at a 45-degree angle and then down to create a mitered corner.

Fold down here.

45° angle

7. Resume stitching, mitering each corner as you come to it.

8. Stop stitching about 3" after you've turned the last corner. Make sure the starting and finishing ends of the binding overlap by at least 4". Cut the threads, and remove the quilt from the machine. Measure a 3" overlap, and trim the excess binding.

9. Place the quilt right side up. Unfold the unstitched binding tails, place them right sides together at right angles, and pin them together. Draw a line from the upper left corner to the lower right corner of the binding, and stitch on the drawn line.

10. Carefully trim the seam allowance to ¼", and press the seam open. Refold the binding, and press. Finish stitching the binding to the quilt.

11. Turn the binding to the back of the quilt, and pin it. (I pin approximately 12" at a time.) Use matching-colored thread to blindstitch the binding to the quilt back, carefully mitering the corners as you approach them. (Turn the front and back miters in different directions to reduce the bulk.) Hand stitch the miters on both sides.

Making and Adding a Sleeve

If you want to display your quilt on a wall, you need to add a sleeve to protect your work of art from excessive strain.

1. Cut an 8½"-wide strip of backing fabric 1" shorter than the width of the quilt. (If the quilt is wider than 41", cut 2 strips, and stitch them together end to end.) Fold under the short ends ¼"; stitch and press.

2. Fold the sleeve in half lengthwise, right sides together. Sew the long raw edges together, and press the seam open. Turn the sleeve right side out, and press again.

3. Mark the midpoint of the sleeve and the top edge of the quilt. Match the midpoints, and pin the sleeve to the quilt with the seam on the sleeve at the top edge, right below the binding. Use matching-colored thread to blindstitch the top edge in place.

4. Push up the bottom edge of the sleeve ¼" so that when the hanging rod is inserted, it will not put strain on the quilt. Blindstitch the bottom edge of the sleeve, taking care not to catch the front of the quilt as you stitch.

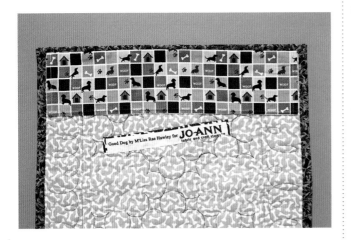

Creating a Label

I always recommend making a label for your quilt. A label gives you a place to provide important information about you, about the recipient, and about the quilt. I like to make my labels large—about 4" × 7"—so I have plenty of room. You can sew the label to the lower right corner of the quilt back before it is quilted or wait to attach the label by hand after you have completed the quilt.

I suggest including the following information on your label: the name of the quilt; your full name; your city, county, province or state, and country of residence; and the date. For a baby or child's quilt, it's a wonderful idea to feature the child's name, along with the occasion (birthday, christening, or other milestone) the quilt was made to commemorate.

Use the label to record key information about your quilt.

You can buy printed labels or make your own simple labels by drawing and writing on fabric with permanent fabric markers. (Stabilize the fabric first with freezer paper or interfacing.) For a more elaborate (and fun!) label, try photo-transfer techniques, use the lettering system on your sewing machine, or use an embroidery machine to embellish your label. You could even create your own distinctive signature or logo. Include patches, decals, buttons, ribbons, or lace. I often include leftover blocks to link the quilt top to the back.

resources

For a list of other fine books from
C&T Publishing, ask for a free catalog:

C&T Publishing, Inc.
P.O. Box 1456
Lafayette, CA 94549
(800) 284-1114
Email: ctinfo@ctpub.com
Website: www.ctpub.com

C&T Publishing's professional photography
services are now available to the public.
Visit us at www.ctmediaservices.com.

For fat quarters and other quilting supplies:

Cotton Patch
1025 Brown Ave.
Lafayette, CA 94549
Store: (925) 284-1177
Mail order: (925) 283-7883
Email: CottonPa@aol.com
Website: www.quiltusa.com

Hancock Fabrics
www.hancockfabrics.com

Jo-Ann Fabric and Craft Stores
www.joann.com

Note:
*Fabrics used in the quilts shown may not
be currently available, as fabric manufacturers keep most fabrics in print for only a
short time.*

For information about thread and stabilizer:

Sulky of America
www.sulky.com

Robison-Anton Textile Company
www.robisonanton.com

For sewing notions and tools:

OLFA
The OLFA® M'Liss Quilters & Crafters Value Kit and other
OLFA products are available at Hancock Fabrics, local quilt
shops and at www.olfa.com.

Embroidery Collections:

My Favorite Quilt Designs, by M'Liss Rae Hawley, Disk Part
#756 253300, **inspira** collection, multiformat CD-ROM

Spring View, by M'Liss Rae Hawley, Disk Part #756 255100,
inspira collection, multiformat CD-ROM

Curious George Adventures, by Husqvarna Viking, Disk
Part #412 6661-02

Dakota Collectibles Collection Volume 20

Applique Fun #F70307

Muppets embroidery designs, Disk Part 5567 251100

Quilting with M'Liss, by M'Liss Rae Hawley, Husqvarna 175

Stuffed animals:

Steiff North America, Inc.
www.steiffusa.com

about the author

Photo by Michael Stadler

M'Liss Rae Hawley is an accomplished quilting teacher, lecturer, embroidery and textile designer, and a best-selling author. She conducts workshops and seminars throughout the world. As the author of twelve books and the originator of numerous innovative designs, M'Liss is constantly seeking new boundaries to challenge her students while imparting her enthusiasm and love for the art of quilting. She likes to break quilting down to the basics, in order to show students that quilting can be easy and fun at any level of skill!

M'Liss designs fabric with coordinating embroidery collections, writes books, and creates patterns for many magazines. She is also the spokesperson for several national and international companies.

M'Liss and her husband, Michael, live on Whidbey Island, Washington, in a filbert orchard. Michael is also a best-selling author and the recently retired sheriff of Island County. Their son, Alexander, is a staff sergeant in the U.S. Marine Corps, currently serving overseas, and their daughter, Adrienne, served in AmeriCorps, is a firefighter, and currently attends graduate school in Dublin, Ireland. Michael and M'Liss share their home with seven dachshunds and four cats.

Great Titles
from  C&T PUBLISHING

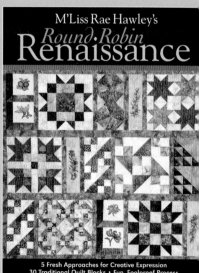